KU-421-145

MEASURE FOR MEASURE:
REFORMING THE TRADE UNIONS

Also in the Reform Series

*

J. P. Mackintosh

THE DEVOLUTION OF POWER:

Local Democracy, Regionalism and Nationalism

THE REFORM SERIES

Measure for Measure:

REFORMING THE TRADE UNIONS

STEPHEN FAY

1970
CHATTO & WINDUS
CHARLES KNIGHT
LONDON

Chatto & Windus Ltd.,
Charles Knight & Co. Ltd.
London
*
Clarke, Irwin & Co. Ltd.
Toronto

SBN 7011 1588 2 (hardcover)
SBN 7011 1589 0 (paperback

Printed in Great Britain by
R. and R. Clark Ltd.
Edinburgh.

Contents

Introduction

To begin a book by revealing its limitations might seem strange, but it is essential in this case. I concentrate wholly on the trade unions, and ignore management–their partners in the industrial relations system. The omission is quite deliberate; the problems of the trade unions alone are quite comprehensive enough to fill this, and other, books. But I would not like the reader to believe that management is somehow immune from criticism when collective bargaining is under attack. Far from it, for the weakness of the unions must reflect a similar weakness in management. But the faults of British management are another subject, and I do not deal with them here.

Nor does this book visualise a society broadly different from the one which exists, however imperfectly, in Britain now. It does propose a new approach to trade unionism, but the approach is designed to fit into and assist the mixed economy as we know, and often misunderstand, it. Probably my most basic assumption is that the unions themselves must change if the society in which they exist is to remain stable. Obviously all assumptions would change in a Socialist or Powellite state, but my own proposals implicitly reject both. Were either to emerge in Britain I would be the first, I hope, to dismiss the proposals I make as irrelevant to a new, and quite different, political problem.

It is with some diffidence that I produced a series of trade union reforms. Working each week in the company of trade unionists, civil servants, politicians and managers, as I do, the subtle shades of grey which inevitably descend on one's conversations tend to obscure any simple formula for reform. I have decided, quite deliberately, to ignore the subtle shades. The result is often over-simplification. No human institution with as long a history as the

British trade union movement can, however, be easily stereotyped. There are rules, but there are as many exceptions to them.

It is not just because I have over-simplified that most of my conclusions will be unacceptable to many of the people I hope are my friends in the trade union movement. They will fundamentally disagree with them. But the attack on the trade unions as institutions is not intended to be an attack on the probity, charm, or wisdom of the trade unionists I know. I am indebted to them, because they have helped me write this book by discussing their problems and attitudes with me.

I have also been greatly helped by colleagues on the newspaper which employs me to spend my time on the fringes of the trade union movement, the *Sunday Times*. I would particularly like to thank its editor, Mr Harold Evans, its Managing Editor, Mr Michael Randall, and the editor of Business News, Mr Peter Wilsher, who have borne with me patiently whilst I tried to evolve a coherent view of the union movement. Another colleague, Mr Eric Jacobs, kindly read the manuscript and made valuable suggestions. But my greatest debt is to my wife, Prudence, who is not responsible for any of the grammatical, stylistic, or logical errors, but who is responsible for the absence of many others. Finally, I unreservedly include the customary author's caveat that the responsibility for all errors, ideas and omissions is my own.

London, August, 1969

I

1906: Legal Immunity

The character of modern British trade unionism was formed in 1906, just three years after the death of Queen Victoria. It can be dated quite exactly. On 14 December, 63 years ago, the Marquis of Ripon moved that the House of Lords pass the third reading of the Trades Disputes Act and make it law. It was a momentous occasion, though it received only scant notice in the newspapers the next day, for the Act confirmed that British trade unions could not be sued in tort for damages by employers for any action of a member of the union during a strike; that, to all intents and purposes, a union involved in collective bargaining is responsible in law neither for its own actions, nor the actions of its members.

The tradition founded that December day on the motion of a Marquis was that British trade unions should be virtually immune from any framework of law limiting their powers and their actions. The Trades Disputes Act, 1906, confirmed the interpretation of an earlier Act, the Trade Union Act, 1871, which stated that agreements between groups of workers and groups of employers are not, in any circumstances, legally binding. So when a union, or an employer, chooses blithely to ignore collective agreements* made between them, there is nothing either side can do to redress the balance except to flex its muscles and try to force its opponents to bow to its will. The effect was to make British labour relations a trial of strength between the two sides of industry, regulated voluntarily by custom and practice, but not by legal precedent.

It is not surprising that the Trades Disputes Bill was introduced at the insistence of the trade union movement. In 1901 the House

* In this context collective agreements are agreements made between employers' associations and trade unions,

of Lords' judgement in the Taff Vale case, in which the Taff Vale Railway Company had sued the Amalgamated Society of Railways Servants, had stated, contrary to all precedent, that unions were liable for damages caused by the actions of their members. What the judgement suggested, translated into modern terms, was that if a small group of members of the Amalgamated Union of Engineering and Foundry workers struck and held up deliveries to the motor industry, their employer could sue the AEF for damages, particularly if their members had, like the railwaymen at Taff Vale, 'induced blacklegs to break their contracts by refraining from strike-breaking'.

The judgement was clearly unacceptable to the unions. It cost them £200,000 for a start, and as the Tory member of Lambeth and Norwood, Mr G. S. Bowles, cheerfully pointed out during the House of Commons debates on the Trades Disputes Bill in 1906, the number of strikes had decreased, and the membership of trade unions was declining as a result of the Taff Vale decision. 'It seems to show clearly what many of us have supposed,' the reactionary Mr Bowles continued, 'that unless a trade union can manage to keep going a certain number of trade disputes, the mere fact that they can offer benefits, the mere fact of all their other activities, will fail to keep together the number of their members.'

But the necessity for freedom to strike was very real. The trade union movement was still in its infancy, despite the laws which had been passed to protect them by Gladstone's administration in the 1870s. Total membership was only two million, recognition was hard to win from the employers, and strikes were often the only method of persuading employers that they had no alternative but to negotiate with a union. More important, employment was hard to get, and, as a result, both trade unions and individual working people inevitably felt insecure. The Taff Vale judgement added to their insecurity, so it was obvious that the unions would use what political power they had acquired to persuade Parliament to reverse it. The unions, with some justification, believed the statement made by one of the Labour members, Mr D. Shackleton, during the Commons debate: 'that the unions are infinitely more free from tyranny than the Primrose League has shown itself in some rural constituencies'.

The unions had their way in 1906; Parliament agreed to abdicate its responsibility for making laws to give the community general control over one of its parts. But the decision did not just establish the character of trade unionism for one brief term of Liberal Government; it has lasted until the present day. And only rarely during the succeeding six decades has a Government tried to reassert itself. The Conservative Party muttered about doing so during the late 1920s, after the General Strike in 1926, but apart from two Acts cancelling each other out controlling the unions' right to finance the Labour Party, no Act has been passed in peace-time which undermines the legal immunity of trades unions. (The Trade Disputes Act, 1965, in fact reinforced that immunity, on which partial doubt had been cast by a judge's decision in the 1960s.)

Only in 1969, when the Labour Government decided to introduce its first Industrial Relations Bill, was the principle of trade union immunity finally questioned, and then only in those selected instances arising from economically damaging unofficial strikes, or inter-union demarcation disputes. But the combined efforts of backbench Labour Party Members of Parliament and the Trades Union Congress successfully defeated the effort by Mr Harold Wilson and Mrs Barbara Castle to curb the immunity granted 63 years earlier. The struggle over the Labour Government's short Industrial Relations Bill in the spring and early summer of 1969 gave the impression that the unions had somehow established a divine right to their legal immunity. The acerbic comments of the Irish Tory, Edward Carson, during the 1906 debates seemed to have been proved right. He had said that a new constitutional theory had been advanced; the Commons knew that the King could do no wrong; now they had decided that the trade unions could do no wrong.

Since the original decision has been so readily accepted for so long, it is worth investigating the circumstances of its origin. The Trades Disputes Act has become the equivalent of the Commandments which were writ on stone on Mount Sinai. The unions regard it with similar reverance and resist with the fervour of the Crusaders any attempt to alter its emphasis. How, then, did it happen?

The fact is that the passage of the first Trades Disputes Act was what Mr George Woodcock would describe as a shoddy, shabby compromise. It was also the first great Parliamentary victory won by the six-year-old Labour Party under the leadership of Keir Hardie. In the 1906 General Election the first block of Labour members had been returned, but there were only 29 of them. During the campaign, however, Labour supporters had successfully badgered Liberal candidates to sign a pledge that they would support a Bill to overturn the Taff Vale judgement and give the unions legal immunity. The Liberals, who had won a massive majority, were almost as good as their promise. In March 1906, only a month after the King's Speech, a Trades Disputes Bill was introduced by the Attorney-General, Sir John Lawson Walton.

In his opening speech in the debate on first reading on 28 March, he announced: 'We will remove the fetter which is placed on (the unions) by the operations of the (legal) action of conspiracy. We will give them permission, so long as they observe the law as it affects individuals, to carry out their own policy.' It was, he added, a more thorny problem than had ever presented itself to a Government. *The Times*, in an editorial the next day, disapproved. 'His Bill goes a long way, most people think a dangerously long way, in exempting trade unions from the law which is to bind everyone else.'

But it was already clear that the Bill had not gone far enough to please the Labour Party. *The Times* described their view unsympathetically, but not inaccurately: 'They object to the pretence that (the Bill) still maintains the supremacy of the law, because they are thereby obliged to say that they did not authorise actions which they wish honestly to avow that they do authorise and approve. They want legislation frankly authorising all they need to do without any attempt to blind the rest of the community to what is going on.'

By a remarkable stroke of luck, a Labour member, Mr W. Hudson of Newcastle-on-Tyne, had come top of the ballot for private members' Bills, and only two days after the Government's Bill was introduced, Mr Hudson introduced Labour's own. It did not, as the Attorney-General's Bill had tried to do, impose minimal curbs on the unions. As Mr Hudson put it, his Bill proposed to return 'exactly to the position in which (the unions) were originally placed, namely, of entire immunity from the law. It is not a matter of privilege, but a matter of right.'

Mr Hudson was followed by a succession of unhappy Liberal members who had to tell their front bench that their election pledges morally bound them to support the Labour Bill. The situation was ludicrous: a Cabinet whose Government had one of the largest majorities in the history of Parliament, seemed to be in danger of defeat only six weeks after it had taken office. Half-way through the debate on Mr Hudson's Bill the overwhelming desire for political survival asserted itself. The Prime Minister, Sir Henry Campbell-Bannerman, rose and told the Liberals to vote for the Labour Bill and sort out the differences between the two conflicting Bills in Committee. He rationalised his sudden about-face by saying that: 'The great object is to place the two rival powers of capital and labour on an equality so that the fight between them, so far as the fight is necessary, shall be at least a fair one.'

Predictably, *The Times*, then a Conservative newspaper of course, was appalled. 'The Prime Minister did not leave the House in suspense, but showed only too clearly that the iron of Mr Keir Hardie's threats had entered his soul.' It was obvious that *The Times* agreed with the Right Honourable G. Wyndham, who made his only intervention in all the long debates on the Bill that year to accuse the Prime Minister of 'a cowardly surrender'. But Sir Henry had his way. The second reading of Mr Hudson's Bill passed with the greatest of ease by 416 votes to 66.

During the summer and autumn, the Labour Party pressed its advantage home. Its Bill was taken over by the Government, and the only amendments passed were to help the unions by legalising the right to picket and to come out in sympathy with other strikers.

The Government tried desperately to salvage as much of its dignity as possible, and in doing so, laid the philosophical foundations of the relationship between Governments and the unions for decades to come.

Sir William Robson, the Solicitor-General, began the process during the second reading when he made the delightfully obvious point that: 'A trade union is more like a public meeting than a railway company.' He rationalised the Government's adoption of the Labour Bill by explaining that the unions had acted with so much prudence and so much moderation in the past that Parliament could fairly and prudently entrust them with the immense and exceptional powers which they demanded. The Tories were unappeased, in debate at least. They attacked the legislation on the grounds that it conferred privilege on a small sector of the community, despite the fact that this had been the reason for their own existence for many years. The Party might no longer believe in the Aristocratic Settlement, but it had yet to embrace social democracy. Since the Tory attack was led by F. E. Smith and Edward Carson, two of the finest debaters of this century, the Government's reputation was badly battered; and their vulnerability was increased by the knowledge that the Chancellor of the Exchequer, H. H. Asquith, the Foreign Secretary, Sir Edward Grey, and the political head of the Army, Lord Haldane, did not like the Labour Bill.

Once the decision had been taken by Campbell-Bannerman it was unalterable, and after gruelling debates, the Bill's third reading was reached in the Commons on 9 November. This historic occasion was conducted largely in the absence of members of either of the front benches. Perhaps they were ashamed of what they had wrought. The Tory leader, Arthur Balfour, did intervene, however, to admit defeat grudgingly. He derived some consolation, he said, 'from the knowledge that Englishmen have shown themselves in the past to be able to use exceptional powers with moderation'. The Tories had decided not to vote against the Bill in the Commons, and the Conservative peers in the House of Lords, who had the manpower to throw the Bill out if they chose to do so, did not fight either. It was the greatest victory the unions in alliance with their new Parliamentary allies had won: indeed, the only one to rival it in this century was a similar alliance's victory in 1969. On that occasion it was a Labour, rather than a Liberal, Government which was humiliated.

Not everyone in the Labour movement was altogether delighted by the conversion of the Liberal Government to the principle of total immunity. In their *History of Trade Unionism*, Sidney and Beatrice Webb say that: 'Some friends of the trade unions expressed at the time the doubt whether the policy thus forced upon Parliament would prove, in the long run, entirely in the interest of the movement; and whether it would not have been better to have chosen the bolder policy of insisting on a complete reform of the law, to which, when properly reformed, trade unions should be subject in the same way as any other associations.'

Asquith, who was to become Prime Minister two years later, made it clear that, despite his late conversion to the Bill, he was not necessarily in favour of a permanent abdication of Parliamentary responsibility. 'When trade unions abuse their powers, Parliament can interfere', he told a Manchester audience in November, 1906. But the extraordinary thing about British trade unionism is that no peace-time Parliament felt impelled to interfere for 63 years, and the additional fear of the Webbs, that the lawyers would not be long in taking their revenge, was not to be justified for 58 years.

Throughout that period collective bargaining in Britain remained entirely voluntary. Only during the two World Wars, and after 1966, when the first Prices and Incomes Act was passed, have the Government had the power to meddle with the outcome of collectively made bargains. Apart from the hiatus immediately before and immediately after the general strike in 1926, it was not until the end of the 1960s that many people in and out of Parliament began to ask the question posed by *The Times*'s leader writer in 1906. 'Can the community feel sure that for all time to come the leaders of the trade unions will be men of the same character and the same calibre as most of them have been until now?'

The question was of course asked regularly by extreme right

wingers who doubted the value of trade unionism itself. But they have always been a small minority, except during the 1920s when many more people were briefly deluded into thinking that the trade unions might be the instruments of revolution. One of the reasons why *The Times*'s question was not asked insistently until the 1960s, is that the unions never intended to become revolutionary organisations. In return for their immunity they certainly did conform. Balfour's grudging optimism in 1906 was misplaced only on rare occasions. They have consistently supported a Labour Party whose emphasis has always been on social democracy rather than socialism, and the Communist Party was not significantly more successful in its attempts to infiltrate the trade unions than it was in its early attempts to affiliate to the Labour Party. One of the many reasons why the ballot-rigging scandal in the Electrical Trades Union in 1959 (finally fought out in the High Court after which the Communist leadership was deposed) was so scandalous, was that it was so rare. It shocked because it cast a slur on the loyalty and patriotism of the British trade union movement, and, after the Second World War at least, that was heresy.

The other factor which prevented the unions becoming a subject of national concern for such a long period has almost been forgotten now, but it is perhaps the most significant of all: they were too weak to assert themselves during long periods in those 63 years.

Certainly they won a victory in 1906, but that was a Parliamentary victory. Its fruits were harvested between 1911 and 1921, when trade union membership rose from 3·1 million to 6·6 million, largely because the Government encouraged recognition in return for wage control and co-operation during the First World War. By then, the unions felt they were strong enough to take on the employers, and, when necessary, the Government. By 1926 they had discovered that they were not. After eight days of general strike the TUC ordered its members to slink back to work, and the miners were left alone again to fight both the Government and the mine-owners.

That experience did the trade union movement no good; the

subsequent Depression did it terrible damage. At the height of the Depression membership dropped to 4·6 million, a reflection not just of the extent of unemployment, but of the unions' impotence. There was nothing they could do about it. There was something else, too, which kept them less powerful than they became after the Second World War: industry was less inter-dependent. A strike in one sector of industry did not necessarily affect other sectors; and, equally important, the spread of public services had only just begun. It was not until the 1950s that great conurbations of millions of people could be effectively crippled by strikes which affected heat, light and transport.

During the Second World War the trade union movement did begin to regain its strength; even then its strength was often illusory. But in war as in peace, the unions insisted that collective bargaining remain free. If limitations were to be imposed, they would be self-imposed. On the whole, the policy was highly successful. Early in the War the first stirrings of a voluntary incomes policy emerged from tripartite discussion between Government, unions and employers. Only towards the end of the war was it thought necessary to bring in restrictions on a few unofficial strikes, and an order permitting compulsory arbitration. These were rarely used, and they were soon forgotten after the war. But this brief experience confirmed all the unions' prejudices against judicial intervention in collective bargaining, and those prejudices have lingered, unweakened, to the present day. Ground once won by the unions is held with great tenacity.

If the prejudices of the unions did not change in the generation after the war, conditions did. A detailed account of these changes, and their effect on the economy and the unions, follows in later chapters, but they can be dealt with briefly here because they explain why a Labour Government, heir to the rump which had so skilfully seduced the Liberals in 1906, decided to reverse the fundamental principle upheld then: the immunity of unions and the partial immunity of trade unionists from legal action.

The one thing that matters most is full employment. The social effects of there being 98 out of every 100 workers in secure employment have been remarkable. More than anything else, it characterised post-war Britain, just as *un*employment did between the two World Wars. Ever since the war-time Coalition produced an economic policy for the peace whose centrepiece was full employment, Governments have never wavered in their determination to keep to that promise. By the 1960s argument about employment had narrowed to a sophisticated debate on the impact of unemployment rates of between 1·5 and 2·5 per cent.

It is still not pleasant for any man or woman who cannot find work, but it is less debilitating, socially and economically, and it has ceased to be the dominant obsession of the unions. At the turn of the century their most important job was simply to try to give a member the security he lacked. Sixty years later, 97·5 per cent of the labour force was secure in the knowledge that it could get work if it wanted. In a way this achievement was partially due to pressure from the unions: they had hammered the need for full employment into successive Governments, and it had been accepted. So had their demands for better social service benefits, redundancy pay, and re-training grants.

Having won these victories, the purpose of trade unionism changed. The behaviour of trade unions did not. They ignored the implications of their victory. If any Government dared to propose a *quid pro quo* for full employment, it went away with a flea in its ear. It must sometimes have seemed that the 1906 Act had created a monster which could no longer be controlled, and as industrial change gradually caught up with social change, the need for control became more and more apparent.

Although a new Britain was not to be forged in its white heat, as Harold Wilson forecast in 1963, there was a technological revolution in the decades after the war. Industry became more complex. Few factories were self-sufficient; more and more processes were dependent on the output of other factories. Yet industrial integration was occurring simultaneously with a process of disintegration in the power structure of the unions. Collective bargains were still being struck, as they had been for decades, at national level between the national officers of unions and national representative of employers, but in many industries they were becoming less and less relevant. All that most national negotiations were doing was to provide no more than a basis for a realistic local settlement in the factory. The trend increased the influence of the local bargainers, and their power, was boosted by the proper fashion for productivity bargaining in the 1960s.

The combination of local power and integrated industry naturally increased the tension between the trade union movement and the Government. The Government is, after all, responsible for economic policy, and the Labour Government believed it saw that policy being threatened by small groups of trade unionists irresponsibly wielding their newly gained power, often in defiance of their own union leaders.

It was union weakness, exaggerated by the apparent abuse of local power, which led to the hasty decision to introduce a short Industrial Relations Bill in April 1969, and it was the strength of the labour movement's conservatism which led to its being dropped only two months later. The argument actually bore little relation to the subject at issue, which was collective bargaining. The Bill was seen instead, as an attack on 'trade union liberties': the same liberties that had been established in the shoddy compromise 63 years earlier.

As in 1906, the victory was a Parliamentary one. So great was the opposition among the Labour backbenchers that the Cabinet eventually told Mr Harold Wilson and Mrs Barbara Castle to retreat with as good a settlement as possible. The settlement, which gave greater powers to the Trades Union Congress, was slightly better than Mr Wilson could have hoped for. But the Labour Party, bound by such strong traditions, had forced Parliament to abdicate its responsibility once again.

In retrospect, however, it is likely that the drama of the summer of 1969 will take on another significance. The Government's decision to try and limit the immunity of trade unions broke a spell which had lasted for decades. The truth of Asquith's maxim – 'When trade union abuse their powers, Parliament can interfere' – was acceptable again. The Labour Party had put the unions on their best behaviour. But it was clear that the Conservative Party could hardly wait to get its hands on them. The Party was also confident that it would receive a mandate from the voters to do so in the next General Election. The importance of the great trade union dispute in 1969 was that it did initiate, albeit very hesitantly, trade union reform. And once begun that is virtually impossible to stop. After 63 years the argument had suddenly changed: it was no longer whether reform should take place, but how and when.

2

The 1960s: Growing Unpopularity

The most significant achievement of the British trade union movement during the fifty years following the passage of the Trades Disputes Act, 1906, was clearly the total confirmation of its legal immunity; and by the middle of the 1950s a convincing degree of political immunity had become associated with the freedom from legal constraints. During the Second World War the unions had been drawn closely into the body politic, after years of exclusion during the pre-war Conservative and Coalition Governments. Sir Winston Churchill, whose Minister of Labour, Ernest Bevin, was drawn from the Labour movement, called the unions 'the fourth estate'; and the description was not unfair, for the unions had by then established a fundamental principle in their relationship with Governments: before policies which affected the working lives of working people were introduced, the trade union movement through the TUC should be consulted.

The object, of course, was to restrain Governments from interfering too drastically with the business of trade unionism–industrial relations and collective bargaining. It was a protective mechanism as much as anything else. Only in selected instances in which the Government might act sympathetically towards trade unionism was their intervention welcomed, and the relationship between the two bodies came to be defined by trade unionists in a somewhat self-absorbed way. Government conciliation in industrial disputes did not count as intervention; to refuse to conciliate did.

This attitude reached its apogee in the mid-1950s when first Churchill's, then Eden's Conservative Governments wanted, above all else in their industrial relations policies, to avoid a clash with the unions. Under the gentle and generous guidance of Sir Walter

Monckton they succeeded admirably, and the period is still remembered nostalgically by some sentimental old Ministry of Labour hands as the nearest approach to Elysium achieved by the department in its relations with the unions. (The view is largely discredited under the present Labour regime, which appears to regard that period either as a joke or a nightmare.)

The most piquant example of Conservative complaisance occurred in 1957, when engineering workers were striking to force the employers to submit to a generous, and inflationary, wage claim. The Ministry, characteristically timid when faced by powerful unions striking to achieve their demands, tried to persuade the employers to give more than they were willing to pay. The employers rejected the Ministry's advice, and won a limited victory in the settlement which followed. The incident was an intriguing reflection on a generation of change. Between 1926 and the outbreak of war the unions had not the muscle to frighten a Government. Now they had.

After the war, the movement did little more than flex its muscles during a sympathetic Labour administration; the Tories appreciated the strength of the unions, concluded they were unable to harness it, and decided simultaneously not to resist it. This combination of attitudes made the strike weapon a fearsome one, and since the Government spent a good deal of its energy dissuading the unions from using it, it meant that their members emerged from wage negotiations with settlements which were satisfactory to them.

A corollary of this situation was that the unions believed they had even more power than they actually had. National officials became over-confident, and they did not seek to control the trend towards substantial local wage settlements, which was certain to grow in a period when economic activity was at a consistently high level and labour was scarce. So the importance of the first shift in the Conservative Party's policy was missed.

In 1958 the newly elected leader of the Transport and General Workers' Union, Frank Cousins, decided to bring the London busmen out on strike. He expected an easy victory, but the new

Minister of Labour, Iain Macleod, was of a different generation of Tories. He felt little or no guilt for the economic mismanagement of the 1930s. He had no debt to pay to the unions for their war-time co-operation as Sir Winston and Sir Walter Monckton thought they had. On this occasion the Ministry of Labour forced the Government to see that it had little to lose by fighting the London busmen: exports were not going to suffer, and it quickly became clear that Londoners could find other methods of getting to work. So the Ministry refused to conciliate on Mr Cousins's terms, and after a seven-week strike the busmen went back to work, defeated.

The bus strike also revealed an unrecognised weakness in the trade union movement. Mr Cousins might well have frightened Mr Macleod off had the railwaymens' union stopped working on tubes and commuter trains in sympathy with the busmen. A few years earlier they might have done so, but a new generation of union leaders were reacting against the traditions created by the comfortable, decidedly reactionary, cabal which had dominated the TUC since the end of the war.

The unions were to be weakened further during a decade in which many of the leaders of the biggest unions on the TUC had a highly-developed antipathy for each other. Frank Cousins, William (later Lord) Carron of the Engineers, and Jack (later Lord) Cooper of the General and Municipal Workers, were never keen on each other's company and even less so on each other's ideas, and significant co-operation between the three largest unions in the country was always formal, never effective.

The shift in the Government's attitude during the bus strike was only one of emphasis. There was still no fundamental change in the Government's attitude towards the unions as such. When Mr Macleod, and later Edward Heath, moved on from the Ministry of Labour to higher, and possibly better, things, and when Mr John Hare (now Lord Blakenham) took over, any progress there might have been from changed attitudes to reformist policies was quickly dissipated.

Sir John was of the old school, a paternal Conservative who

delighted in the cosy relationship he was able to convince himself he had created with leading trade unionists. Trade union leaders had become 'chaps', and with the sad exception of one or two angular and abrasive figures, they were all 'good chaps'. It was not an atmosphere conducive to constructive criticism, let alone self-criticism, and it led to the development of a remarkable state of mind: few people in Government or the unions ever questioned *the system.*

At the beginning of the 1960s there was no conspiracy to prevent serious discussion of trade union reform. It was not necessary for men to plot to prevent the Government, or anyone else, interfering with the system. Certainly, there were damaging restrictive practices; obviously, there was serious over-manning; clearly, a vast majority of the wage-payment schemes were archaic, and bore no relationship to work performed in modern industries; it was true that the structure of the unions was clumsy; that they were obstructive on vital, but unpublicised, matters such as apprenticeship and training; of course productivity could be a good deal higher; there was, indeed, too much over-time worked; admittedly the unions sometimes appeared to allow political obsessions to overwhelm their primary industrial activity; it was, perhaps, true that the quality of trade union officials was declining as more sons of the working class were better-educated and went on to university instead of the shop floor; and trade union salaries did fail to keep up with those earned by some of the men they represented; it was true, too, that the authority of the general council of the TUC was declining, and power was passing more and more to shop stewards, who were for the most part unregulated and unrecognised. All this might be true but the system was, nevertheless, 'the best in the world'.

'The system' was Britain's voluntary method of collective bargaining, in which excesses were recognised, but largely dismissed as the product of an insubstantial minority. Change would come, the uncritical admirers thought, through the institutions which the voluntary system had developed to regulate itself. Only ten years ago so many people in Britain believed that their system was the best that to propose radical change for the unions was thought to be rather crankish. More, there was a subtle suggestion that criticism of the trade union movement was somehow unpatriotic.

The unions were rather like Britain's commitment East of Suez and the existing parity of Sterling. Both were institutions reflecting the greatness of Britain's past, and they must be clung to if Britain were to remain great in the future. Because the British trade union movement was the first to develop it was felt that it must reflect inherent strengths which others, developed later, lacked. And since those other movements–the American, the Swedish, the Australian–lacked the stability of the British trade unions, it was therefore understandable that those foreign Governments should feel the need to pass legislation which controlled their union movements more vigorously than in Britain. In its purest form, the argument implied that British democracy depended on an unreformed system of industrial relations. British democracy, after all, developed the system; so to change that system was to erode democracy. The statement was a false syllogism, whose nature was not to be realised for some time; sadly, many trade unionists still believe it to be true.

But in less than ten years that assumption has crumbled, and the argument has begun to wither away. During a remarkable period which began in 1961, the unions have been attacked with increasing bitterness, and during the 1960s they became a target for abuse from all sectors of the political spectrum. Some of the criticism was so bitter that it became irrational: there were people who convinced themselves that if only the unions could be reformed, all the nation's problems would somehow dissolve. The sacred cow became a black beast.

This transition was probably inevitable. The immunity from fundamental criticism, which the unions had nurtured for so long had become a habit, and when it was finally questioned, those who had accepted it suddenly discovered that they had been duped. The natural response to that condition is anger; the natural result is an unseemly, and sometimes ugly, barrage of abuse. The wonder is that the unions managed to survive the 1960s unreformed.

After some vacillation, Harold Wilson's Labour Government decided that other sacred cows had to be sacrificed first: the East of Suez commitment was finally demolished in 1966; and in 1967, after 18 months suffering from a deluded conviction that Sterling at $2.80 equalled virtue, the Pound was finally devalued. The unions, however, were not reformed, they were merely interfered with. Proposals for trade union reform finally emerged from the Government only in 1969, at which point the tide of virulent abuse which had been directed at the unions was suddenly turned on the people trying to reform them.

It was a confusing period, and it is not easy to impose an order on it. But one thing must be explained: why, after so many years of immunity, had the sacred cow become a black beast? Why were the unions singled out from so many other British institutions to bear the burden of so much sensate and insensate anger? There is, in fact, a single answer which is better than all others: it was because of the atmosphere of permanent economic crisis which closed in on the country in 1961, and which, at the time of writing, has yet to lift.

On 25 July 1961 Selwyn Lloyd, the Conservative Chancellor, introduced the first of the interim Budgets which were to characterise Government fiscal policy during the decade. But this one contained something different. Mr Lloyd demanded a freeze on wage increases which lasted until 1 April the following year. It was the first occasion on which a peace-time Government had interfered so comprehensively with collective bargaining. The cause was one which became familiar as the years passed: the balance of payments. The reserves had been dwindling for six months, and the Government had to act to contain the losses. Mr Lloyd decided that a conventional credit squeeze was not enough, and concluded that the Government should begin to use its power as an employer to set the pattern for other wage-increases. Civil servants' and public employees' wage increases were to be stopped.

Mr Lloyd's policy was based on a complex theory, but its outcome was simple: it forced the Government to intervene more and more in wage settlements. The economic problem underlying balance of payments crises was inflation and economic analyses in the late 1950s had offered two explanations for it. One was called 'demand pull'. It suggested that the most effective way of dampening inflationary pressures was to deflate the economy. Deflation was supposed to have the effect of increasing unemployment, reducing the shortage of labour, and, therefore, curtailing the power of the unions to bargain hard for substantial wage increases. The alternative theory was called 'wage push', and it suggested that high-wage settlements were the primary inflationary influence which was pushing the nation towards the abyss of a permanent balance of payments crisis. By the beginning of the 1960s the wage push theory had become accepted wisdom in the Treasury, and it was to dominate successive Governments' economic policy for years to come.

The reaction of the unions to Mr Lloyd's wage freeze was predictable enough: a sense of outraged self-righteousness was felt in trade union branches throughout the land. There was talk of taking the Government to Court to contest the legality of its policy, by unions which resisted in principle the intervention of the law in collective bargaining. But their biggest stick of all was never used: the dominant unions did not harness their industrial power to break the freeze. The electricians' union did manage to make the freeze look less than complete, and the civil service unions showed that they could be angered into talk, if nothing else, of the use of force; but the railwaymen were bought off by one of Harold Macmillan's most spectacular political *coups*. He persuaded them that to strike to break the freeze would be an affront to the memory of the men who died at Passchendale.

The freeze was a partial success, since wages went up by only 2·2 per cent during its existence. More significant, however, was that it came at a turning point in modern economic administration. At the same time the Conservative Government began to flirt with ideas which implied more direct control over the economy. Reginald Maudling, at the Board of Trade, was half-heartedly playing with a regional policy which was designed to reduce the impact of industrial under-development in Scotland and the North-East of England. Shortly afterwards Edward Heath was to interfere in manufacturers' pricing policies by ending resale price maintenance. The decision to intervene in wage settlements was in the same mould. But the Government did not have the political courage to act on their analysis. They were still afraid of the unions, whose ability to bluster and bully was, if anything, growing greater. Just as a full-blooded policy of intervention to attack regional unemployment was an affront to the traditions of private enterprise decision-making, direct intervention in wage-bargaining would spoil the comfortable relationship that the Government had built up with the unions.

But Selwyn Lloyd's freeze also demonstrated that the unions were either unwilling, or unable, to put their money where their mouth was. Their opposition was moderately effective, but they were reluctant actually to employ the strength people believed they possessed, to overthrow a policy they despised. Some were inclined to attribute this reluctance to the maturity of the unions, but in fact their strength was somewhat illusory, and certainly not as great as the Government feared. As if to demonstrate the fact, in the summer of 1962 unions in the engineering industry ballotted their members to discover whether they would strike to force the engineering employers to improve an ungenerous offer, and the workers turned the proposal down with startling alacrity. Trade union power at the centre was diminishing fast; on the shop floor, of course, it was growing. In industrial sectors where the unions had never been strong, the low-paid could see no real hope of radical improvement.

Because it did not have the courage of its convictions, the Government decided to pursue a policy of consensus: its Ministers were not inclined to act unilaterally, and they seemed still to believe that the unions had the power to act out a positive co-operative role in the first crab-wise steps towards economic planning. (The French, it will be remembered, had made planning respectable in the previous five years.) The instrument of consensus in industrial politics was to be the National Economic Development

Council, which announced, in the middle of 1962 (shortly after its first meeting), that an agreed growth rate of 4 per cent a year was to be programmed for the British economy.

For the next four years the economy was to a great extent conditioned by the attempt to achieve voluntary consensus. The unions were to be given their opportunity to define the national interest (a verbal argument embracing one of George Woodcock's favourite obsessions); and if the unions' ability to deliver what little they promised was doubted privately, it was accepted at face value in public. But they still retained the appearance of controlling the kind of destructive force which made any alternative to consensus unthinkable. When the Government, in another half-hearted effort to restrain wage increases, decided to introduce the National Incomes Commission, the unions simply refused to co-operate. But the NIC was a singularly inappropriate institution, run like a Court by a skilful and respected lawyer, Sir Geoffrey Lawrence, whose insistence on everyone's standing as he and his Commissioners entered the room, and on no-one smoking while he took evidence, raised the hackles of the few sympathisers NIC ever had.

The drawback of a policy of consensus in industrial politics is that it assumes, and desperately needs, a high rate of economic growth to support it. Reginald Maudling, who had succeeded Mr Lloyd after Mr Macmillan's Cabinet putsch in 1962, grasped this. In 1963, he initiated a period of rapid growth which, for two years, kept pace with NEDC's 4 per cent a year target, after the two years of economic stagnation which characterised Mr Lloyd's administration. Mr Maudling's policy was the fashionable one; the Labour Party was staking all on it, and the unions were equally enthusiastic about it. It was, after all, necessary to support the high levels of public expenditure to which Mr Wilson and his colleagues were committed. But the cost was to be seen in the balance of payments figures. In 1963 the deficit was £110 million; in 1964, during the final months of Conservative Government, and the first two months of Harold Wilson's administration, the deficit exploded to £747 million. It was these statistics which finally affected the fate of the trade unions.

The brief period of economic growth had been accompanied by a steadily upward trend in wage settlements, and Mr Maudling had made desultory and unsuccessful attempts to get the unions to accept an incomes policy of wage restraint. Despite the level of growth–the *sine qua non* for the policy's acceptability to the unions–incomes policy became a symbol of Tory rule, and the unions rejected it with the vigour of pressure groups fighting a political campaign–which, of course, they were.

As Labour's administration began it should have become clear that the vain attempt to achieve a consensus between the Government, the unions and management had failed. Logically, the only alternative was direct Government intervention in wage bargaining, but the Labour Government shied away from it, just as their predecessors had done. The unions kept up the pressure for inflationary wage-settlements, in spite of George Brown's flamboyant efforts to persuade them to do otherwise. Indeed, in the first year of Mr Brown's voluntary incomes policy, earnings rose at a greater rate than at any time during the decade. Deflation seemed to be the inevitable corollary. In 1965 the growth rate slipped downwards to 2·7 per cent; by 1966, when the most vigorous deflation since 1949 was introduced, it had fallen to 1·5 per cent. In each of these years, the declining growth rate was accompanied by a balance of payments deficit–£227 million in 1965, and £99 million in 1966.

The apparent intractibility of the economic crisis led the Government in a desperate search for remedies. Mr Wilson, Mr Brown and Chancellor of the Exchequer James Callaghan, had rejected devaluation. It might well have worked, but if devaluation was out, a wages policy was obviously in. So the Government directed the emphasis in its economic policy towards the bargaining process and the unions. An early-warning system had already been established and Aubrey Jones was appointed to run the new Prices and Incomes Board. Its first job was to apply moral suasion, that wasting asset in a modern economy, on unions which were pressing too hard for wage increases.

Soon afterwards the TUC were persuaded to undertake voluntary wage-vetting of claims, but it was clear from the outset that the policy was unlikely to work. The affiliated unions were too unsympathetic to allow it a chance. To make matters worse, the incomes policy was allied to another poor thing: Mr Brown's National Plan, an exercise in planning which will be remembered as one of the most ambitious and meaningless documents to emerge from Whitehall during the 1960s.

By the middle of 1966 it had become clear to all but the unions involved in it, that the voluntary system of wage-bargaining did not have long to last. And the unions' failure to implement any satisfactory method of controlling wage increases was exacerbated by another act of trade union intransigence–the seaman's strike–which finally triggered off the worst of a succession of balance of payments crises, and led to a wage freeze which made Selwyn Lloyd's look like an experiment in Tory freedom. The seamens' strike, even though the union had a worthy case, reduced public sympathy for the unions even further; and the episode had one other significant side-effect. It taught Harold Wilson that there seemed to be massive electoral advantage in abusing the unions. In succeeding years he did not hesitate to act on that knowledge.

The wage freeze which followed the frenzied miscalculations in July 1966 was the most successful of the decade. For the stability of the British economy in succeeding years it was, perhaps, unfortunate that two factors combined to make the freeze so effective. Many trade unions genuinely seemed to feel some remorse for the remarkable wage-increases their members had been getting during the previous 18 months. They even backed Mr Wilson's policy at the TUC Congress, which followed only six weeks later. That remorse, combined with the first legislation to give a Government statutory power to delay wage increases–the Prices and Incomes Act, 1966–led Mr Wilson and his colleagues to believe that a rigorous attack on wage inflation might be the solution to their economic problems. During these months the conviction that the 'wage-push' theory was right probably reached its peak. It was not until late in 1967 that an alternative analysis was finally accepted.

In November Mr Wilson's Government finally concluded that

the currency was overvalued, and devalued the Pound by 14·3 per cent. But the effect of a freeze, followed by severe restraint backed by legislation, had already taken its toll. The remorse of the unions did not last that long, and although none of the large unions ever fought the Government's policy by means of their bluntest weapon, the national strike, they kept up a consistent offensive against the legislation, especially after its renewal earlier in 1967. This appeared to harden the Government's determination to concentrate on incomes above all else. Despite their insistence that the policy was applied to prices as well, only the most unimaginative Party loyalists were convinced.

Another effect was becoming clearer as the months went by. When the Labour Government had first tried to sell its incomes policy, Ministers had argued that it was an instrument of social justice. So it can be, when the economy is growing rapidly and incomes can be redistributed without higher-paid workers taking too much umbrage. But by 1967 and 1968 the idea of social justice was being talked of less and less (although it did revive briefly late in 1968 after Barbara Castle took on the Department of Employment and Productivity).

What happened was that the rich got richer and the poor got poorer. Skilled and semi-skilled workers in factories where union organisation was good were negotiating sizeable increases. And the Government could not, or did not dare–in the case of the dockers, for instance–to stop them. In industries in which organisation was poor, wage levels which were already low moved up very slowly. So slowly, in fact, that improved social security payments were making it hardly worth some men going to work for their money.

As the economic crisis worsened, confusion multiplied. Britain's economic problems seemed to become more and more intractable, especially after devaluation failed to produce the expected improvement in the nation's prospects, and the search began, not for a solution, but for a target. What better target than the unions?

The evidence was available in abundance. During the years of the primacy of incomes policy, the unions had obstructed efforts to control the rise in wages, so that the Government had been forced to strengthen its policy of interference in collective bargaining. The unions had failed, when the opportunity was presented to them, to accept the TUC's voluntary wage-vetting policy. They had, in fact, failed to realise just what a parlous state the economy was in, and this failure had actually added to the crisis. It was, and still is, a damning indictment. But one of the reasons for the unions' intransigence was the feeling, which became a fear, that they were being isolated: that when blame came to be distributed, they would be given more than their fair share.

During 1968 the Government's opposition to the trade unions began to change. They needed a new explanation for the miserable balance of payments position, and with the publication of the Donovan Report (formally known as *Royal Commission on Trade Unions and Employers' Associations*) in June, they found it. Unofficial strikes became the new target; after all, 95 per cent of all strikes were unofficial, Lord Donovan's Commission reported.

The Government grasped at the fact that this meant that some unions had lost control of some of their members. Unofficial strikes were a growing irritant, and their growth had coincided with incomes legislation and restraint. Union leaders, having decided not to attack the policy frontally by striking nationally, were quite happy to see the policy subjected to guerilla attacks on its flanks by groups of unofficial strikers.

As the Government's obsession took its grip, the incidence of serious unofficial strikes actually grew, particularly in the motor industry. By the end of 1968, strikes had become a source of national despair. By April 1969, when the Chancellor of the Exchequer, Roy Jenkins, delivered his Budget, the transformation in Government policy was complete: incomes policy had virtually been forgotten; the emphasis had shifted to legislation designed to intervene and curb the strike weapon.

And so the decision to reform was taken, although it was to be frustrated two months later. It was tentative, and it had taken a long time; it took eight years to wear down belief in the political immunity of the unions to the point at which their legal immunity could be questioned and, indeed, attacked. Though during the economic crisis the unions had changed, they had not changed enough to satisfy the hunger for reform which the crisis had initiated. Despite hundreds of productivity deals, there were still damaging restrictive practices, in defence of which the engineering unions, particularly, indulged in damaging strikes. Over-manning was still rife. Many of the wage-payment grades were still archaic and troublesome; and the structure of the unions had changed little in spite of a considerable number of amalgamations during the decade. The Government's intervention in training had helped a good deal, but no real progress had yet been made on problems connected with the length of apprenticeship. Despite countless deflations, overtime was still common in industry; and the introduction of legislation to control wages and curb strikes, had increased the amount of time devoted to political rather than industrial activity. The quality of trade union officials had not improved notably over the decade, and it was also true that, though power had continued to pass to shop stewards in the factories, few serious attempts had been made to recognise and control their activities.

Since 1906 the trade union movement had been irresponsible in the sense that it was in no way responsible to the community at large. After the war, their freedom grew, and so did their uncontrollability, which certainly contributed to the economic crisis in the 1960s.

The extent of that crisis never really gripped trade unionists in the old-fashioned way which so many of them remember so vividly. There was never any serious unemployment, except for the winter of 1962–3, when the weather was so bad that it was surprising that unemployment was not worse; and what unemployment there was was made more bearable by better social security benefits. Nor was there any serious interruption in the slow, but steady, rise in the standard of living. With the single exception of poor housing, which meant desperately large numbers of homeless and badly housed people, the majority of the complaints against Government took on a decidedly middle-class tone: the health service was not good enough; schools were overcrowded and the facilities were poor. These, valid as they were, were not the complaints of a broken working-class.

Economic crisis was reflected in balance of payments figures, statistics showing the drain on Britain's currency reserves, and the level of the nation's indebtedness. And figures of that kind do not strike terror in the breast of 'the ordinary working' man. So the crisis in no way limited the irresponsibility of the unions; and it was the most obvious symptom of that irresponsibility–the all too frequent unofficial strike–which finally spurred the Government on to attempt trade union reform.

3

Strikes: Power Abused

There was nothing new about criticism of the British trade unions' propensity to strike unofficially. Gnomish commentators abroad had been shaking their heads for years, though for most of those years the British themselves had just shrugged their shoulders. The strikes were part of 'our way of life'. The Ministry of Labour complacently bolstered this attitude by pointing out Britain's relatively low position in the international strike league table, and it was not until the economic crisis had become another part of our way of life that their attitude began to change.

There was, of course, something in those foreign criticisms, though not as much as bankers in capitals throughout the world affected to believe. Bankers as a group still tend to question the basic principle of the right to strike. If Governments weak-mindedly accept it, they argue, those Governments should certainly curb it. There was something else that foreign bankers, and, indeed, some commentators in Britain itself, did not understand: the tendency of the British press, to exaggerate the impact of strikes on the economy.

In his tendentious pamphlet *Is Britain Really Strike Prone?* published in May 1969, Bert Turner, the Montague Burton Professor of Industrial Relations at Cambridge University, suggested that newspapers were partially responsible for the newly-developed British obsession with strikes. 'One reason,' he wrote, 'is undoubtedly a seeming public preference for the disastrous in its taste for reportage of any kind. . . . From the point of view of the mass media, good news is no news, and the effect of the selection of the satisfyingly catastrophic is to project the abnormal behaviour as the norm. Data chosen for its sensationalism, however, is an extremely poor basis for policy.'

It is true that newspapers, in Britain and elsewhere, do tend to report more bad news than good news; it is more memorable. When newspapers report good news, it is quickly forgotten; and newspapers reflect the tastes and tendencies of their readers, rather than impose these on them. To rise to Olympian heights and ignore that fact is to court the danger of non-communication. But Professor Turner nevertheless had a point. To invest it with real significance he would have had to have more sympathy for the structure of the British newspaper industry.

The difference between the British press, and newspapers in the United States, Germany, France, Italy, and most other major industrial nations, is that it is nationally, rather than regionally based. In the United States, during the seven-week dock strike in the East coast ports during the winter of 1968–9, the crisis never took on the air of a disaster partly because the coverage of the strike was, for the most part, scattered. There would be small paragraphs most days on the particular state of affairs in the port in which a newspaper was published. It read like a local affair, whose effect on the nation, the economy and the balance of payments was negligible.

In Britain, the reverse is the case: a local strike in Liverpool attracts national attention, and becomes an issue of national scandal and concern. There have been few national strikes in Britain during the past decade, but many thousands of strikes have been fully reported in national newspapers. A strike at Rootes' motor factory in Linwood outside Glasgow, when channelled through newspapers sold all over the world, can evoke outrage in New York and Detroit. And there is, incidentally, a reasonably well-paid group of specialist journalists who are hired to exploit this situation.

The result, however, is not distortion, as Professor Turner would have us believe, but exaggeration. The alternative would be the situation revealed by a West German representative of the Confederation of British Industries. In Germany, he explained proudly, if something goes wrong at a factory, there is a conspiracy (my word, not his) to prevent it from becoming known to the world at large. The news is, in effect, censored, and it is an attitude which corrupts. The British taste for 'the satisfying catastrophic' (to quote Professor Turner) might be troublesome, but it makes Britain a more open society.

Professor Turner believes that there is a case of distortion, however. The press, he seemed to be saying, had inflicted its private views on Lord Donovan's Royal Commission, the Conservative Party, and finally the Government. All, he claimed, were guilty of taking strikes too seriously. Pages of his pamphlet were devoted to proving that the small unofficial strike was not particularly damaging, especially when its impact was compared to strikes in the United States. The cost of these small strikes, the Professor concluded, was minimal–maybe 'considerably less than 0·1 per cent of all time worked during the average year'.

Some areas of Professor Turner's argument are indisputable. Certainly, the fact that 95 per cent of all strikes are believed to be unofficial is not, in itself, a justification for treating the business with great gravity. Certainly, it is true that 75 per cent of the strikes reported to the Department of Employment and Productivity last no more than one day; that 89 per cent last less than four days, and that only 4·6 per cent of all strikes last more than 12 days. So a good many unofficial strikes can be dismissed as a mere irritant.

What the Donovan Report argued, however, was that they were a symptom, rather than just an irritant: that they have an effect on morale which cannot be quantified, as Professor Turner's case can be, on logarithmic scales. When managers are convinced that change will provoke a strike, it reduces their desire to introduce change. Professor Turner claimed 'that the average manager' is likely to be confronted by a strike 'not more than once in 20 years'. This could be construed as an adverse comment on the quality of British management as well as a positive proof of the rarity of strikes in Britain.

Statistics can be used to prove anything, and to bolster any case. It would appear that both the Department of Employment and Productivity and Professor Turner were over-enthusiastic in using the same figures to justify totally opposite conclusions: one claimed they made law necessary, the other that they made it redundant.

But hidden away in the mass of statistics there are figures which tell us what the strike problem is, even if they do not suggest how it should be dealt with. They are also published in the DEP's monthly *Employment & Productivity Gazette*, and they demonstrate that the 4·6 per cent of strikes lasting for more than 12 days were responsible for 35 per cent of the aggregate number of working days lost during all strikes in 1968. Narrow the figures down and they become even more dramatic: 1·4 per cent of the number of strikes in 1968 caused 18·2 per cent of the aggregate days lost during the year. The statistics suggest, as Professor Turner did, that the problem is not one concerning the small strikes. But there is, none the less, a very considerable problem: one of the strike which lasts, and has a multiplier effect throughout industry, and throws men who are totally uninvolved out of work.

The enthusiastic commentaries on Professor Turner's document after its publication never grasped this fact. A cursory reading of Professor Turner's pamphlet does give the impression that strikes do not matter. But the Professor, having dismissed the strike problem, actually goes on to define it rather well. Three-quarters of the way through, his argument is suddenly interrupted by a statement of the obvious: 'all this is not to say,' he writes, 'that *no* strike–whether big or small–has any important economic effect.' Shortly afterwards, Professor Turner, the champion of the trade unionists and those politicians who opposed the introduction of strike-curbing legislation, makes a startling admission. 'Since balance of payments constraint has been a major pressure towards restrictive Government measures which have kept the level of employment at a higher level in recent years than formerly, that is, in the writer's view, perhaps one strong case for special additional measures in relation to industrial disputes.' That was the same assumption underlying the Government's hesitant attempts at trade union reform in 1969–the very reforms which triggered Professor Turner's attack. It is a correct assumption, and to try to destroy it by applying general and national strike statistics is to introduce a crude red herring. Britain's strike record might be exaggerated, but a few serious strikes have symbolised the malaise which overshadows the nation's industrial relations. They offer the sharpest explanation of why reform is necessary.

The Government's White Paper, *In Place of Strife*, which was published in January 1969, rightly stated in its very first sentence that: 'There are necessarily conflicts in industry.' The object of a policy for industrial relations must, equally necessarily, be to reduce the conflict, and to channel what conflict is inevitable into more orderly, less destructive, patterns of behaviour. The trouble with British strikes is that too many of them are disorderly, and a few are destructive–not just of the balance of payments in the short-term, but of the status of the trade union movement too.

The disorder creates confusion, which naturally makes a rational analysis of the problem more difficult. Confusion has arisen, for instance, about the fundamental purpose of strike action. Traditionally it has been thought of as 'the final sanction', a course which is undertaken only when verbal negotiation through established procedures has completely broken down. The theory is rather different from the practice, for many strikes, particularly the brief and unofficial ones, are merely used to interrupt the verbal process. Often they do not even strengthen the bargaining position of the union representatives. When people complain that procedures are being ignored, they usually mean that the strike is being used as an intermediate, rather than a final, weapon. Such strikes are unpredictable, and the fact that the managers have little or no warning of them must reduce their morale.

But there is another important respect in which the practice is different from the theory of industrial relations. Both the Donovan Report and the Government's White Paper emphasised that unofficial strikes comprised 95 per cent of the total of something between 2,000 and 2,500 strikes every year since 1955. The lesson to be learned from these statistics, they both suggested, was that bargaining power had moved from the national union centre to the shop floor, and that national union officials had lost control of the bargaining process.

This is, perhaps, too simple an explanation, and Ben Roberts, Professor of Industrial Relations at the London School of Economics, has questioned it. He argues that many unofficial strikes are, in effect, official, because they are silently, if not formally, sanctioned by the chief officers of the union. It is an attractive theory because it bears some relationship to social trends which affect strikes in Britain. The strike benefits paid by most trade unions are pitiful sums, fixed years ago, and still unchanged because few unions collect large enough dues to finance a large strike fund. The £3 10*s*. a week paid by the engineering union is not enough to keep most of its striking members in the Midlands, for instance, in beer, cigarettes, and petrol for a week. Most families are helped during a strike by social security payments to the wife and children of the strikers, and these payments rightly cushion the impact of a strike; as do tax rebates. They tend to make demands that a strike be made official less pressing; and they do, therefore, tend to make the relationship between 'unofficial' strikers and their national officials more complex.

It did not take this additional complexity to resolve the thousand doubts, and dispel at least some of the fears, which dominate any attempt by Government to undertake a programme of trade union reform. When the Department of Employment and Productivity decided late in 1968 to try and push ahead with reform sooner than Lord Donovan's Royal Commission had recommended; and when Barbara Castle and her Government colleagues decided to go even further, even faster, in the spring of 1969 by proposing immediate legislation to curb strikes, each decision was influenced by a major strike. The first was at the Girling factory in Bromborough, Cheshire, owned by Joseph Lucas Ltd., which supplies vital components to the motor industry. The second was the strike which closed the Ford Motor Company for four weeks in February and March 1969. Both appealed to Mrs Castle's taste for quick and melodramatic intervention.

Two strikes might seem an insubstantial platform on which to base the first great attempts at trade union reform in 63 years. To claim that they were the sole basis is, obviously, to exaggerate. But the Girling and Ford strikes are classic examples of the failure of the system, and the need for reform. At certain points during each, the two strikes dramatically illustrated a variety of weaknesses in the trade union movement: the frivolousness of some shop steward decisions; the incompetence or myopia of some national trade union leaders of great eminence; militancy of leaders at both local and national levels becoming an end in itself; the weakness of management; a total intolerance of the law among trade unionists; the ridiculous inflexibility of different unions towards their members' jobs on the factory floor; and the inadequacy of long-established negotiating procedures. The strikes are worth observing in greater detail.

The Girling factory in Bromborough, which is in western Cheshire, is, perhaps significantly, not far from Merseyside, one of the great cockpits of British industrial warfare. The factory employs 2,000 men and women, and makes caliper disc brakes for motor-cars. On Monday, 11 November 1968, the Alphing section –known as section 204–came to a halt. The stoppage was caused by the management's decision to send home five setters (men who set up the production machine ready for the production operatives) because they had refused to take a supervisor's order to turn on a tap which would supply oil to the production machines. Twenty-two other setters in section 204 then walked out in sympathy. Once they had stopped work, production immediately stopped in the section; the rest of the 400 workers were laid off, and brake production ground to a halt. So dependent are large sections of the motor industry on the production of brake linings at Girling that, as the strike wore on, 5,300 men were laid off at Ford and Rover factories. It took 29 days, and a Court of Inquiry set up by the Department of Employment and Productivity, holding three full days of public hearings, to get the 27 men back to work. It was a classic instance of the damage a few men can cause to a massive industry; and it was, tragically, a storm in a teacup from which it is difficult to extract either principle or common sense. It illustrated what the Bank of International Settlements was to describe the following June as 'a tinge of anarchy in British labour relations'.

The trouble was that the shop stewards belonging to the

Amalgamated Engineering and Foundryworkers Union, which dominates the engineering industry, had not only won great power, but that that power had run out of their control. As the pages of evidence to the Court of Inquiry reveal, no one could exercise any real influence over the Convenor of Shop stewards, Ted O'Rourke, and a group of his colleagues. A. J. Nicol, Joseph Lucas's deputy managing director told the Court: 'We are incapable of controlling a small group of AEF stewards, but Mr Hearsey's officials (Arthur Hearsey is an executive councillor of the AEF) are incapable of controlling them too; they never follow procedure.'

Of course, Mr Hearsey denied the charge, but the evidence bore it out. Communications had broken down, and in the preceding 10 months there had been 57 disputes in the factory, 33 of them in section 204. The management was not even sure who the AEF stewards were, since the local district officer of the AEF had not told them. Some difficulty had arisen because of this, the factory's personnel manager admitted. 'There are quite a number of stewards who claim to be stewards-elect, but they cannot show evidence by showing their stewards' credentials,' he said sadly. The result was that the slightest spark could ignite a dispute of a size disproportionate to its cause. The personnel manager's diary for 21 March 1968 illustrated just one of these disputes: '4.15 a.m., Scott Alphing setter found asleep in the rubber room by night superintendent and dismissed. All setters stop work.' Stop work, it would appear, for that fundamental trade union principle–the freedom to have a kip on the job.

The ostensible cause of the 11 November dispute was inter-union rivalry. There were six chargehands, the first line of supervision, in section 204. In September four of them had joined the burgeoning white-collar workers' union, the Association of Scientific, Technical and Managerial Staffs, whose general secretary, Mr Clive Jenkins, is one of the most successful recruitment officers the British trade union movement has ever had. One other chargehand had applied to join the ASTMS, and only one of the six was a member of the AEF. The ASTMS was accused of poaching members from the AEF, and there is, indeed, some evidence that the union had cut corners in signing up the men, not all of whom, however, had previously been members of the AEF. A plant agreement signed in 1967 gave the AEF negotiating rights for those chargehands who belonged to them. A national agreement with Joseph Lucas gave the ASTMS rights to negotiate for any chargehands who joined them.

In September 1968, Girlings granted recognition to the ASTMS, It sounds like a perfectly straightforward operation; it was, in fact, remarkably hazardous. Early in the proceeding Mr O'Rouke had accused one of the ASTMS men of stabbing him in the back, and, as the Court's proceedings quoted one eye-witness, he added: 'whether there are witnesses present or not "I will get you".' Now there is a method by which Mr O'Rouke could have 'got' the ASTMS. It is called the Bridlington procedure, a system set up in 1939 at the Bridlington Congress of the TUC to ensure the amicable settlement of inter-union disputes by independent, trade union arbitration. The local officials of the two unions were well aware of the procedure; both sides had agreed that there was dispute about membership and that it should be dealt with by national officials of both sides.

In the factory a two-week agreement had been reached in October between the men and the management, in effect, freezing the dispute. When it ran out AEF stewards voted by 23 to 1 not to demand sanctions against the ASTMS chargehands, and it was agreed that Mr Hearsey would visit the factory on 14 November to discuss improvements in industrial relations. He was too late. They had deteriorated three days earlier to the point at which an order from an ASTMS chargehand to turn an oil tap, a job which setters had done regularly in the past, was refused. The strike had begun. On 14 November Mr Hearsey did appear and discuss the problem and within forty minutes he and a local ASTMS official had arrived at an agreed interim solution: the chargehands would not have direct responsibility for supervising the setters while the dispute was being sorted out. The next day the strikers rejected both Mr Hearsey's advice and the formula. The stoppage continued.

It is possible, even likely, that in its enthusiasm to recruit new members, the ASTMS was in breach of the Bridlington agreement. But there is no doubt that, in their rejection of advice from a national official, the AEF strikers were in breach of the Bridlington agreement. And it was clear that the AEF had no means of persuading them to accept the terms a national official had speedily hammered out, and go back to work. The strikers were unmoved even by a letter from the AEF executive, sent on 22 November 'strongly advising them to go back to work'. Mr Hearsey explained to the trade union representative on the Court, Mr John Bothwell of the railways clerks union, 'In the holiness of the TUC procedure, what you say–that we have ignored Bridlington–is correct. In the unholiness of what is happening at Girling brake factory, the answer is that we are unrepentant.'

It would have been a disappointing remark for any TUC supporter present at the hearing, and it was not a good augury for the new strike-settling procedures the TUC was to adopt in 1969. It suggests that the AEF thought that Girling was so special that the rejection of TUC procedures could be easily contemplated, and it was possible to sense that the strike was not simply an inter-union dispute from Mr Nicol's despairing statement: 'If we had not had *this* dispute, we would have had another.'

Minute 204/68 of the Wirral and West Cheshire District Committee of the AEF on 13 November 1968, two days after the strike began, gives a clue to extent of the breakdown in industrial relations. In the Minute, Mr O'Rourke offers another explanation for the dispute. The battle with the ASTMS supervisor is dismissed as 'a further incident' rather than the central cause. On Friday, 8 November, management at the Girling factory had issued an order which prevented setters taking showers during working hours. This had sometimes been considered necessary because the oil made them dirty, but showers had been locked because someone had damaged them. Shower curtains had been torn down, and, as a management representative at the court reluctantly and delicately put it, someone had defaecated in the shower. It does not reflect well on the man who did it; nor does it reflect well on the management which took the consequent decision without consultation. But it does seem strange that a strike which brought sections of the British motor industry to a halt when it was trying to benefit from devaluation in export markets, should begin because one man shat in a shower, and another refused to turn a tap.

Each explanation of the Girling disaster comes back to the same underlying weakness: the structure of the AEF, the predominant union at Bromborough. There was no real communication between the stewards, who knew the local situation, and the local and national officials, who could put it into context. The fact that the ASTMS had substantial membership in other Lucas factories, and that Lucas recognised the union as a negotiating agent, must have been irritating to the AEF stewards at Bromborough, but they could hardly reject its significance.

There were, additionally, serious personality problems in the factory. As the Court of Inquiry pointed out, human failings were just as important as procedural omissions. 'The AEF shop stewards, singly or collectively, in this part of the Girling factory ... appear to have displayed an intemperance of manner and a stubbornness of attitude which have made industrial relations difficult.' It suggests that the stewards represented the workers at the factory less well than they could have done. (This was certainly the implication made by a courageous lady member of the General and Municipal Workers who interrupted the Court's proceedings.) If this was the case, then the union officials at local and national level were certainly too passive in allowing the stewards to have it all their own way against what was admittedly a weak, fearful, but often stubborn, management. The leadership, locally and nationally, did not lead. On the contrary, in one of the most interesting commentaries on the role of elected union leaders, Mr Hearsey told the court: 'I am paid by my members to serve my members, and my job is to satisfy them, not for them to satisfy me.' In other words–'My members right or wrong.' It was a suitable epilogue to a sad affair.

The strike at the Ford Motor Company's factories in February and March 1969 showed that Mr Hearsey's definition of trade union leadership is not held by all his colleagues. At Ford, the leadership was decidedly active, with the members satisfying the leadership, but the results were no less disastrous, both for the 38,000 men and women involved in the strike (out of 46,000 Ford employees), and for the economy generally and the balance of payments in particular.

The Ford strike had a variety of causes: a different one was offered at each stage of the dispute. Sometimes it appeared to be about the balance of power on the negotiating body, the Ford National Joint Negotiating Committee (NJNC), at others about a claim for parity of earnings with motor workers in the Midlands. But it ended, as it began, as a dispute about Ford's insistence that, in return for lay-off pay when the factories were stopped by strikes outside the control of the company or workers, or by economic inactivity, bonuses would depend on good industrial behaviour. If a man had struck unofficially in the six months prior to a lay-off, he would not be eligible for it. These sections of the agreement were called the penalty clauses, and they were a precursor of the desperate opposition that was to follow two months later when the Government introduced its short Industrial Relations Bill.

The Ford strike is less well documented than the one at Girling; there was no Court of Inquiry at which the assumptions of both sides were exposed and questioned. The negotiations took place behind closed doors, and both sides struck public attitudes that were often as misleading as they were unconvincing. This account is not intended to be an exhaustive secret history of the Ford strike; it does, however, trace a few of the most significant strands in the argument.

The first sign that there might be trouble at Ford's had come more than three months before the strike actually occurred. Although the negotiations had been conducted at a speed rare in industrial relations, these things inevitably take months to germinate. Ford had concluded the previous autumn that two things must be done: it had to pay the men more money, and it had to try and reduce the lightning strikes which interrupted production in a highly integrated and complex industrial process. Late in November

1968, they tentatively offered the unions the 'no-strike bonus'. It was a radical proposal, one which was bound to lead to trouble unless it was explained by men sympathetic to the idea. But a large majority of the members of the trade union side of the negotiating committee took the decision to keep the company's plans secret, and not tell their members.

It was not an unusual decision; trade union officials often behave as though they are members of a closed society, from which most of their members, as well as press and public, are excluded. But as negotiations become more complicated, the arguments in favour of greater consulation become more convincing rather than less. In large factories like Ford, there are invariably politically-motivated men whose divine mission, like the Irish trade union leader, Jim Larkin, is 'to preach discontent'. Unless the shop floor workers know exactly what is happening, it is ridiculously easy for them to become misinformed. This is what happened once the trade union side of the joint negotiating committee had decided in November on secrecy. When there are 18 unions represented on the committee, as at Ford, it is naïve to believe that none of the union representatives will leak a version of the proposals.

Reg Birch, the AEF's representative on the Ford committee, whose behaviour was to become curiouser and curiouser during the dispute, was accused of giving details of the proposals to some shop stewards, and the campaign against what were immediately named the penalty clauses began at once, before substantial negotiations were opened. It is likely that had the shop stewards at Ford been officially informed at an earlier stage, there would have been less trouble. The argument within the factories would at least have been less emotive, and more evenly balanced. Once the majority of the trade union officials had decided to conform to their traditional patterns of behaviour, trouble was bound to break out over an agreement whose conception was radical, if not exactly revolutionary. It introduced new principles, and the old procedures were not made to persuade workers to consider the offer in the spirit in which it was being made.

It is possible that the members of the trade union side of the negotiating committee were so busy discussing the plan among themselves that they forgot about their members; there were certainly enough people to keep the conversation going for weeks. It is difficult to find a negotiating body which is quite as anachronistic as Ford's. All 18 unions with members at the factory–from the Transport and General Workers, with 17,500 members, and AEF with 15,000 to the Blastfurnacemen and the Metal Mechanics with less than 100 each–were entitled to representation on the committee; and when a decision had finally to be taken, it was on the principle of 'one union, one vote'. Traditionally, the smaller unions defer to the two dominating unions. A small working party hammers out an agreement and presents it, *fait accompli*, to the other members of the committee. But that system is based on one important assumption: that the TGWU and the AEF agree to the offer, and can persuade their members to accept it.

After some hesitation, during which the company was persuaded to increase the price of the deal which would give them the 'no unofficial strike' agreement they so desperately wanted, and to drop penalty clauses from sick pay agreements, the unions seemed to decide they were ready to agree. But the system was too fragile to bear the strains which were then inflicted upon it. The TGWU man, Leslie Keeley, said he would have to wait to see if the new deal satisfied his unhappy shop stewards; and the AEF man, Reg Birch, having attacked Mr Keeley for hesitating, voted in favour of the agreement going to the full committee and then, in full committee, proceeded to vote against it. If he wanted to reject it, it seems reasonable that he should have done so in the working party. It is impossible to discover what Mr Birch's motives were, but his action certainly created endless trouble, because the smaller unions on the committee outvoted the giants who could have prevented the vote being taken at all. After the favourable 7–5 vote was announced, Ford assumed, incautiously, that they had a deal.

Within two weeks they were to discover that not only had they no deal, they had the threat of an official strike by a newly formed alliance ('we'll strike if you will') of the two largest unions in the company, if they introduced the agreement accepted by the vote of the NJNC on 1 March. Ford's negotiators admitted privately that the constitution of the NJNC was a poor thing, but they stuck to it and the strike began. Then Leslie Blakeman, the leader of the Ford team decided to refer the case to the courts.

Mr Blakeman's decision seemed at the time to be fatal, for it gave the outraged striking unions the opportunity to multiply their claims. As soon as the decision to test the agreement in the Courts had been taken, the negotiations became the property of the leaders of the two unions, Jack Jones, then the general secretary-elect of the TGWU, and Hugh Scanlon, the AEF's President. The fight against the 'no-strike bonus' became a fight against the penal clauses proposed in the Government's White Paper, and the wages issue became a fight for that Holy Grail of motor workers outside Coventry and Birmingham: 'Parity with the Midlands'.

The fact that wages in Ford's main industrial complex at Dagenham lagged behind the earnings based on high piecework prices in the Midlands had always nagged at Mr Jones and Mr Scanlon. Now they had their opportunity to play on the anger and confusion created by Mr Blakeman's decision, and push for Midland rates while the going seemed good. The decision to take the case to the Courts was an inexplicable one, which Mr Blakeman later regretted. It was based on the belief that there is nothing in trade union law which prevented a company, as opposed to a group of employers, making a binding contract with a trade union or group of trade unions. Ford's lawyers argued that the slim 7–5 majority on the negotiating committee (later, for obscure reasons which led to Mr Keeley's resignation from the TGWU, it became an 8–5 majority) constituted an agreement, and that the agreement was legally binding. He was asking the Courts, therefore, to instruct the TGWU and the AEF to order their members to go back to work.

As a case in law rather than industrial relations it was fascinating. Counsel for the AEF, Morris Finer, Q.C., appeared at one point to have brought off a brilliant legal coup when he introduced as a precedent a case heard early in the reign of Queen Elizabeth I involving New College, Oxford, which stated that agreements are not binding in law unless they are unanimous. When Mr Justice Geoffrey Lane gave his judgement, however, it became clear that the startling precedent was irrelevant: the fact that both parties had not intended the agreement to be legally binding was enough to convince him that it was, in law and in fact, not so.

But the occasion revealed more than that. It demonstrated why the unions feel so suspicious of the law. In the first place they are afraid of it. Because they have little experience of the law and the courts, they are bad at judging their chances of victory. Even on the last day, in the middle of the judgement when it was quite clear they could not lose, many senior AEF officials were sure that they were going to. The procedure, the formality, the arrogance of the law is foreign to them; they see industrial negotiation being conducted in upper middle class accents by men in ridiculous garments and wigs, and they mistrust what is going on because they are not certain they understand it. The attitude may be irrational, but it goes very deep.

The more the unions exacerbated the dispute, the more the company determined to stand by its principles. It was a rare case in which the bluff of the leaders of the two largest unions in the country was called; their opportunism eventually reduced their credibility. Shortly before the spate of talks which led to the settlement began, Ford had decided that its losses were so great that they were not worth cutting, and concluded that if winning the strike meant bearing its cost for another three weeks, the cost would simply have to be paid. Neither Mr Jones nor Mr Scanlon could afford a similar price. They must have suspected that the loyalty of their membership would begin to erode after three weeks–there is no other explanation for the defeat they suffered when they finally negotiated a settlement with the company.

It was a humiliating business. Mr Jones at one point attacked Mr Blakeman: he was an underling, unlike the members of the trade union side, and he lacked a managing director's authority, he said. Mr Blakeman assured Mr Jones that he had complete authority. Then when a settlement was agreed, Mr Jones proceeded to astonish everyone by stating that he himself did not have the authority to commit the TGWU to it. He would have to refer to a delegate meeting.

But one thing emerged with great clarity. Ford got the agreement relating, holiday, if not lay-off pay, bonuses to the incidence of strikes, and although the bonuses were higher than when the negotiations began, the terms were slightly more onerous. The unions had fought the principle of penalty clauses and lost; they had demanded parity with the Midlands, and got nowhere. They had alienated a public whose support they needed to fight the proposals in the Government's White Paper, which proposed curbs on the right to strike. Instead, the unions actually tempted the Government to proceed at a faster pace with its proposed reforms, and precipitated the clash which was to sour relations between the two sides shortly afterwards.

The two strikes illustrate a point made by George Woodcock, speaking on the BBC in 1959, just before he became general secretary of the TUC. Talking about trade unions and public opinion, he gave a premature commentary on the Girling and Ford disputes. He argued that: 'If some trade unionists begin to act as though they have no responsibilities to a wider trade union movement, or even if other trade unionists think that they are acting in that way, then there will be no wider movement. The public would not stand for the unions if they felt they were becoming instruments of oppression, and the danger that the unions have to guard against is that the public will turn against the unions to such an extent as to demand that the unions should be restricted from outside–by laws which restrict or prohibit activities which are ridiculous or oppressive. Many of these, but particularly the ones I have mentioned–unofficial strikes, demarcation disputes, noisy demonstrations and the closed shop–are not part of the official policies of responsible trade unions. They are usually the actions of a small group in a factory or workshop.

'In many cases the responsible officers of the unions whose members are concerned dislike these things, and, more important, could stop them if they were determined to do so. In any case I believe that they should make the effort, for it is neither fair to the bulk of ordinary trade unionists, nor wise in the interests of the trade union movement as a whole, to allow an undisciplined minority to get the unions a bad name.'

Ten years after that broadcast it had become clear that undisciplined minorities had got the unions a bad name, but more significant, the responsible officials of the unions were often no longer able to stop them, no matter how great their determination. This was better illustrated at Girling than almost anywhere else during those intervening ten years. But the Ford strike showed that it was the union leaders who were sometimes acting 'as though they had no responsibilities to a wider trade union movement'. Their opportunism overcame their good sense. When the public began to sense this, the Government's obsession about the effect of strikes spread like cancer. And the incidence of strikes in the late 1960s led directly to a crisis of confidence inside and outside the trade union movement, which made it ripe for reform.

4

Leadership: Weakness Multiplied

One of the most intriguing effects of years of full employment is the changed relationship between trade unionists and their unions. In the inter-war period when unemployment was out of control and the unions were under attack, the membership was united. They were a large beleaguered minority in society, and men joined unions to receive what protection they could get from the worst excesses of an economic system which failed them.

Full employment eroded that unity. Trade unionists began to dissociate themselves from the institutions which represented that old beleaguered minority–their unions. They did this not by deliberately resigning from the union–it was too integral a part of their lives, and most members of a conservative working class naturally resist change of so major a kind–but by growing apart from their unions. They formed part of that amorphous mass of 'public opinion' which attacked the irresponsibility of striking workers in the motor industry and the docks. By the end of the 1960s it was no longer surprising to hear a man dressed in overalls or a uniform moaning about trade unions in much the same terms and tones as their traditional middle class opponents.

This subtle change in relationships had two significant results. It meant that groups of workers acting unofficially, sometimes in defiance of their union, were often excoriated by large groups of their fellow workers. The wildcats became more isolated, and simultaneously, as technological change made industry more interdependent, their power increased.

But the disaffection of many trade unionists from their movement also isolated their leaders. The power of national institutions, the huge London-based unions, and, even more so, the Trades Union Congress, diminished. When the unions met in conference, decisions which might have had some impact in years before seemed less and less significant. At the Labour Party conference, the pattern was set in 1960 when Hugh Gaitskell, fighting for his political life, impolitely informed Frank Cousins that the 1,000,000 votes he was about to cast against the Party's official policy did not represent 1,000,000 Labour votes in ballot boxes at election time: if Mr Cousins could get his members to vote Labour with the same facility as he cast their block votes the more likely it would be that he, Gaitskell, would listen to him.

Later in the decade Harold Wilson put the case more succinctly when one of the Government's policies was rejected by the block votes of the big unions at an annual conference. What did the Government propose to do about it? he was asked. 'Govern,' he replied. The same atmosphere of delusion was attached to votes at the Trades Union Congress demanding the nationalisation of this and that. As the decade wore on, the feeling grew that delegates to Congresses and Conferences were talking more to each other, sometimes even to themselves, than to the mass of their membership, or even to sympathetic onlookers in Government.

The process alienated everyone. The stewards on the shop floor began to take less notice of national officials and their decisions; and as the official influence over the stewards diminished, the criticism from outside the movement grew in volume. The one effect magnified the other. By the end of the decade the power and influence of trade union leadership often looked very hollow, and although it perked up under the threat of Government legislation, it did seem to be its tone rather than its character which had changed.

This pessimistic analysis of the leadership of the trade union movement does not mean that the minds of all its leaders were closed, or that no one recognised what was happening or tried to alter the trend. The fact that outside conditions were changing meant there was always a small core of trade unionists thinking harder about the ways in which the movement should adapt itself; certainly there were more thoughtful men in evidence during the 1960s than at any time since the war. The clash between the mass of men who believed that the tenets of trade unionism had somehow been writ on stone and were unchangeable, and the men who knew it must change soon, was nowhere better defined than within the Trades Union Congress itself. It was unfortunate that changes which originated in the TUC had to be based on the assumption that the unions were strong and their leaders able. Nevertheless, there is no better place than the TUC to observe the ideals, the idiosyncracies, and the myopia of the leadership of the British trade union movement.

The history of the TUC for nine-tenths of the 1960s is the history of George Woodcock's general secretaryship. He initiated more reformist ideas than any previous general secretary of the TUC, and his tragedy was that the general council failed to react to those ideas. As one of the older members said after Mr Woodcock had left: 'It was marvellous sitting there and listening to him explain a problem and telling us what to do about it, but it was all talk, he never did anything else.' The trouble with the general council was that they failed to realise that, having accepted Mr Woodcock's analysis and solution, it was their responsibility to do something about it.

So, in spite of the ferment of ideas which Mr Woodcock originated, the member unions of the TUC benefited little. But Mr Woodcock had, in nine years as general secretary, undermined some of the more entrenched positions held by secure trade union leaders, and when, after he left, the threat of Government legislation forced the TUC to begin to think about radical alterations to its attitudes and to its constitution, the ideas themselves were not new–Mr Woodcock and his officials had been playing with them for years. It was the reaction of the general councillors to them which was new. They had been prodded by the Government with a ferocity which Mr Woodcock himself, formally their paid servant, was never able to manage. The irony is that, had they acted on Mr Woodcock's advice earlier in the decade instead of simply listening to it, the debâcle over Barbara Castle's short Industrial Relations Bill might never have occurred.

Mr Woodcock became general secretary at an opportune moment. By 1959 the character of the TUC was undergoing a sea-change. Its orientation was becoming more economic and social. At Congress many of the great debates both before and after the War had been about international relations: Spain and rearmament before the War; the Cold War and the Bomb after 1945. It reflected a somewhat Palmerstonian approach to trade unionism at the centre. Collective bargaining, it seemed, would take care of itself; the rest of the world needed some guidance.

But by the early 1960s Governments had begun to intervene more and more in economic affairs, and the idea of economic planning, long sought after by the unions, was becoming increasingly popular. There was an argument about the character of planning, though. Should it be by decree, or consent? Mr Woodcock's most fundamental conviction was that it should be by consent, and that the unions, through the TUC, should play a central role in the planning process. In return, the unions would behave 'responsibly'. It would mean voluntarily curbing some of their freedoms, but it would make them part of Government in its broadest sense, in a plural society. This would give the Government of the day, and unions, greater moral authority, and would also increase the power of the TUC.

It was because he believed in this radical alteration to the philosophy of trade unionism that Mr Woodcock made his famous speech to the Blackpool Congress of the TUC in 1962. Fortunately there was a motion stating: 'That it is time the British trade union movement adapted itself to modern conditions.' The literal interpretation of the motion was that a programme of structural reform should be undertaken. Mr Woodcock expanded the theme. 'It is not wholly a matter of structure,' he said. 'Structure is a function of purpose. We shall expect to inquire first into our purposes. We must ask ourselves: "What are we here for?" When we have an answer to that, then we can examine our structure.'

Later in the week, he outlined his definition of purpose, during a debate about the TUC's decision to join the National Economic Development Council. The decision was under attack by some unions, which believed that association with an offspring of the

Conservative Government was a trick designed to undermine the Labour movement. 'Are you so scared,' thundered their general secretary, 'that you are not willing to stand by your experience and responsibility? I would rather be a dog and bay at the moon than be such a trade unionist. . . . We must not as a trade union movement give the impression that we want complete freedom, and to hell with everyone else.' It was Mr Woodcock at his best, but his general philosophy implied one particular responsibility, and not even his most cogent Congress speeches could break down opposition to the idea of an incomes policy. It was after all impossible, at that time (and possibly at any other) for Mr Woodcock to argue in favour of direct TUC involvement in economic planning without admitting that one inevitable feature of a plan must be the regulated growth of incomes.

The TUC was then being quietly pestered by the Conservative Chancellor, Reginald Maudling, and the NEDC and staff, for a commitment to an incomes policy. A year later, at the Brighton Congress, the first tentative commitment was proposed. Incomes, a TUC document stated, should rise no faster than productivity. This simple assumption, an essential element in virtually all economic plans, was rejected by enough of the leaders of the nation's influential trade unions to make it inoperative. It was a period in which Mr Maudling was making his so-called 'break for growth' by recklessly expanding the economy and ignoring the consequences. But its success was dependent on the Government's ability to control rising incomes. They could not, and the TUC would not. That failure did severe damage to Mr Woodcock's ambitions for the TUC, and the damage was done in a most unpleasant way.

Many trade union leaders were just as frightened as the mass of their members at the idea of radical change, and that was what Mr Woodcock was proposing. His plan was that the unions should work with any Government, Conservative or Labour. The idea was not immediately attractive: the Conservatives had been responsible for the depression between the Wars, and they were still thought of as 'the enemies of the working class'. It was a fear which Mr Woodcock, a confident man who felt able to take care of himself in any company, rejected, though he understood it. At its worst it produced a miserable exposition of the view of the unions from a man who preached socialism with unremitting vigour. 'If there's going to be a free for all, we're going to be part of the all,' Frank Cousins announced. It was a doctrine of selfish materialism, and it was no compensation to low-paid members of the British labour force–even members of his own union–that Mr Cousins believed in a millenium in which Labour would rule for the benefit of all working men. It was, however, a useful rationalisation for the members of Mr Cousin's union, the Transport and General Workers, who had the local economic power to force employers to disgorge large wage increases.

The semi-skilled car workers in the Midlands and the dockers in London really were part of the 'all'. They were able to force through the kind of wage agreements which increased differentials between themselves and other working men. It was an attitude which corrupted the trade union movement. The unity went. No unions came to the aid of the others in distress, the miners and the railwaymen, for instance, when their memberships were being decimated by modernisation. The reflex action to events had become a selfish and materialistic one, and Mr Woodcock could do nothing to resist it.

He often appeared to be the leading pragmatist in the trade union movement, but that description is unfair. He was, in fact, one of the leading socialists in the movement. He believed that unions should combine, and use their power to help their weaker colleagues. One of the purposes of incomes policy was to help build a national economy in which the local government workers, and the tailors and garment workers, the women workers, even engineering workers outside the main centres of production, would have a fairer deal. The object was social justice, although a secondary object obviously was the expansion of the authority of the TUC. But the outcome of Mr Cousins's materialism was widening inequalities of income, and a reduction in the influence of the TUC.

One more reason why the unions refused to accept an incomes policy in 1963 and 1964 was the proximity of a General Election. A good socialist like Mr Cousins could justify his opposition to Mr Maudling privately on the grounds that a successful Conservative economic policy would hinder Labour's election chances in 1964. (And there was some truth in the claim too; the election was so close that Labour won it finally by stressing the gravity of the economic situation on the electors. The balance of payments was in a precarious position; it would have been less bad had an incomes policy been working in the previous 18 months.)

If Mr Cousins's opposition had been based on political expediency, it would have been more understandable. But, as George Brown was to discover in the first 18 months of Labour Government when he ran the Department of Economic Affairs, the opposition went deeper than that. The fact was that the big unions–the Transport Workers, and later the engineers–simply did not want to see their own already questionable authority dissipated any further. Towards the end of the decade the Government itself became cynical about the TUC's ability to control wages. The movement had moved; by 1965 it was willing to accept, albeit ungraciously, the concept of voluntary wage-vetting by the TUC. It was even willing to vote for the notion that claims in the annual wage round should be submitted to the TUC and placed before the employers simultaneously, on the Swedish model. It got a resounding majority at one of the Conferences of trade union executives in Croydon, which sanctioned the TUC's economic policy in the second half of the decade, but it got no further. The will to push it was not there.

By the end of the decade the ability of the TUC's economic department to analyse the multiplicity of problems in the British economy was greater than at any time in the TUC's history. But it seemed as though the members of the general council, and the Congresses had accepted their own impotence. They had annual economic reviews which, acted upon in unison, might have influenced the economic policy of the Government. They accepted the reports, but without enthusiasm, and since their own lack of enthusiasm was so obvious, the Government could hardly be expected to treat the TUC's economic policy with any more energy. By 1969 it was doubtful whether a majority of the general councillors had actually read the economic views they were recommending first to the annual meetings at Croydon, and then to Government. An opportunity carefully presented to them was thrown away.

The sad fact was that the general council never really grasped the importance of economic policy. Only incomes policy directly affected them; it impinged, to a greater or lesser degree, on their real jobs, as bargainers. At no time were the general council of the TUC willing to see incomes policy in the broader context of economic policy, and of their relationship with the Government. The Government in turn did not assist them to do so. Although many Ministerial speeches explained the policy in terms of social justice, the policy actually contained only a meagre element of such justice. A united trade union *movement* might have fought for an incomes policy that did help the lower paid, even if that help was partially at the expense of higher paid workers. But the movement was not united. The strong ignored the policy, and the weak suffered by it.

This lack of unity was a dominant theme in the TUC's history during the 1960s. It was reflected in the bitter battles between the right and left wings of the general council, like the continuing quarrel between Frank Cousins, leader of the left, and right-wing figures like Lord Carron, President of the Amalgamated Engineering Union. Disunity sapped the energies of the general council to the point at which it was unwilling to act in cases which cried out for the strength unity gave. It produced, for example, one of the least impressive incidents in the decade before Harold Wilson and Barbara Castle tried to transform the character of the TUC.

It was a small strike in Yorkshire, which began in 1963 at the milltown of Baildon, and it involved 300 members of the National Union of Dyers, Bleachers and Textile workers, one of the smaller affiliated unions, but one of the largest textile unions. They had been summarily dismissed after a brief walk-out. The union's general secretary, Len Sharp, was a member of the general council. He appeared to have a good case, which certainly got better as the management became more intransigent and began to hire blackleg labour. The strike stretched on for 16 months. It was a clear case in which a united effort by the trade union movement would have assisted the union, and Mr Sharp asked the general council for help. He asked for months on end. Anyone who could be useful was asked, through the TUC, to strike in sympathy. But not all of them would, and those that could were unable to prevent a determined management from finding blackleg labour to make deliveries, and maintain the machines.

It was clear to anyone who cared to glance at the situation that the strong were unable or unwilling to come to the aid of the weak. It was an example, publicised monthly by the sight of Mr Sharp's face as he emerged from the general council meetings, of the trade union movement's apparent determination not to deploy its strength. Mr Woodcock tried to establish some kind of unity, but he refused to bully the general council. 'Woodcock could talk to them until he was blue in the face,' said one of the people who watched him trying to persuade the general council to become a less passive trade union institution, 'until he asked them to do something, then they would tend to open their mouths to say no.'

Towards the end of the decade, however, there were signs that attitudes were changing. The general council did seem willing to take on more responsibility, but in the main case in which they did so–the dispute over recognition for white collar unions in the steel industry–it is doubtful whether they actually grasped the implications of what they were doing. The bitter wrangle in the steel industry gave the TUC a bad name because it seemed to be a case of the big unions ganging up to protect the established steel trades union (the Iron and Steel Trades Confereration) against the growing incursions of unions like the Supervisors, Technicians and Scientific Workers (ASTMS), and the Clerical and Administrative Workers (CAWU) into an industry in which they had previously been small fry.

The dispute, which began as soon as the industry was nationalised in 1967, was exacerbated by some decidedly hesitant and inconsistent labour relations management by the British Steel Corporation (whose labour relations director, Ron Smith, had been recruited from the general council). The white-collar unions wanted national negotiating rights for white-collar workers and foremen. The Iron and Steel Trades Confederation, which had found it difficult to organise white collar workers in the private steel industry because many employers outflanked them by establishing staff associations, wanted to extend its near monopoly of non-craft trade union membership in the industry.

A Court of Inquiry could not resolve the problem, nor could an investigation by the TUC's own Organisation Committee. So in January 1969 the ISTC decided to take the matter into their own hands and refuse to take orders from members of the ASTMS and the Clerical Workers. If the threat had been carried out, the industry would have stopped production soon afterwards, and it was withdrawn only after Mr Woodcock, and his assistant general secretary, Victor Feather, promised a new inquiry and binding arbitration.

Mr Woodcock's investigation found in the ISTC's favour, and was accepted by the general council: the established union was to have the right to organise and be recognised by the Steel Corporation. It meant that the TUC would support the ISTC in any action it took to implement the award. It was, Mr Woodcock insisted, a judicial decision, and the unions were committed, morally and industrially, to ensure that it was carried out. It was a precursor of the promises made by Mr Feather and his colleagues to the Government later in the year, but the reason so many outsiders were sceptical about the greater powers allotted to the TUC was that the general council gave no indication in the steel case that a binding judicial decision had been taken. The dispute dragged on through the spring and summer much as it had done before.

Perhaps the most characteristic document to emerge from the TUC before it was provoked into writing its radical *Programme for Action* in the early summer of 1969, was its evidence to Lord Donovan's Royal Commission. This was published in a document simply entitled *Trade Unionism* in 1966, many months later than it should have been. When it did come out it was immediately clear that the evidence had not been worth waiting for. It was a long document with a simple message: hands off the trade unions. It was a perfect expression of the views of the general council. The evidence was at its best in its draft form, since it then contained some interesting ideas about the extension of worker participation in industry, but by the time this section had been mauled by a committee of the general council it had been reduced to the banal level of everything else in the document, which stated, for example, that: 'Other countries are increasingly looking to Britain to discover how to evolve a system of good industrial relations.' The irony was lost on the TUC.

One of the reasons for the disaster was that Mr Woodcock partly did not, and partly, because of a heart attack, could not, throw his full energy into its production. He had already badgered the Minister who established the Royal Commission, Ray Gunter, into giving him a place on it. He was able to fight for his view of trade unionism from the inside, so the effort to persuade the Commission from the outside by means of the TUC's evidence naturally took second place. It was clearly too much to expect the TUC's evidence to the Royal Commission to give even a tentative answer to the question posed by its general secretary four years earlier – 'What are we here for?' The strongest theme to emerge from the document was that the trade union movement was there to obstruct.

Nor was the TUC able to achieve much to change the structure of the trade union movement, which was looking more and more anachronistic as the years passed. Mr Woodcock had hoped that a redefinition of the relationship between the unions and the Government would lead to changes in the structure of the unions; but the relationship did not really change. Structure was not altogether forgotten, however, and series of conferences took place under the auspices of the TUC to probe new ways of rationalising it. It would be unfair to say that these had no effect. Mr Woodcock himself preached the advantages of merger and rationalisation to many of the small unions, and Victor Feather worked enthusiastically in the background to bring them to fruition. But the effect of their activities was unfortunately undramatic.

The character of the effort was well illustrated in a meeting of unions in the port industry to discuss closer working and possible amalgamation. Mr Woodcock told them it would be no bad thing and explained why. Then Bill Lindley, a small, cheerful Cockney who is general secretary of the charmingly named Watermen, Lightermen, Tugmen, and Bargemen's Union replied. He astonished his small delegation by speaking at length on the benefits, the delights even, of amalgamation. His colleagues started to mutter that Mr Lindley had no remit to say that sort of thing; that their union, with its 3,500 members, had a tradition of independence which it was unwilling to trade. Then Mr Lindley reached his punchline. Since his union was so knowledgeable about the dock industry, he said, the Watermen were willing to consider a takeover of the massive docks group of the Transport and General Workers Union. It was very witty; indeed, his colleagues retail the story with great glee. But it was the kind of frivolous attitude which makes strong men weep, and it characterised the TUC under Mr Woodcock's general secretaryship.

It was not that Mr Woodcock misunderstood the nature of trade unionism, or the challenges which could undermine it. On the contrary, he was more aware of them than any of his contemporaries, and his speeches during the decade were full of foreboding for the future of the movement. As early as 1959, in the BBC talk quoted in the last chapter, he pointed out: 'When one thinks of the power the trade unions have today compared with any time before the outbreak of the last war, it surely does not seem in the least surprising that nowadays many of the particular activities of trade unions receive more attention and more criticism from the general public than they used to. In other words the trade unions have lost the general sympathy the public usually reserves for the underdog; and the reason for this is that the trade unions do not now give to the public the impression that they are underdogs any longer. With full employment and good trade the unions reckoned they would be able to look after themselves. But that is what the public think too–except that the public is beginning to ask if the unions are not rather too well able to look after themselves.'

Mr Woodcock's analyses were ignored, as were his proposals. And in ignoring them, the trade unions seemed to justify the growing volume of criticism aimed at them. Power was passing from the leadership of the unions to the rank and file membership, Yet the leadership closed their ears to all the schemes proposed by Woodcock which might have helped them correct that growing imbalance. Even when the TUC finally did react positively, in the summer of 1969, to prevent the Government from introducing penal clauses in a new Industrial Relations Bill, their reaction was still based on the traditional desire to obstruct. And with the experience of the previous 10 years of TUC activity, few people had much faith in the TUC's power to activate its promising plans.

5

Organisation: Conservatism Compounded

Rule 15, clause 3 of the rule book of the Amalgamated Union of Engineering and Foundry Workers states quite firmly that: 'The executive council's hours of business shall be from 9 a.m. to 5 p.m., with one hour allowed for dinner, Mondays to Fridays. But in cases of emergency they may be called on to finish thc business in hand. Each member of the executive council shall devote the whole of the business hours to the duties of his office . . .' In capsule form, it says a great deal about the second largest trade union in the land. There are rules for every eventuality, even if they are not all religiously adhered to. Members of the seven-man executive have, in fact, been known to take more than one hour for dinner ('lunch', to the journalists and business men who entertain them), but, to give them credit, they regularly work after 5 p.m., and they do not always finish work on Friday. Still Rule 15, clause 3 implies that the members do not really trust them. The AEF is a craftsmans' organisation, founded by sturdy, independent-minded men who thought that if a leadership was necessary at all, it had to be carefully watched.

A description of the AEF tends to become an entertainment, rather than an analysis. As a union it espouses many of the virtues of Victorian working men; as an organisation representing a vast majority of the men and women who work in the diverse British engineering industry, it is, unfortunately an archaism. In few British institutions is change so resolutely resisted. The mere suggestion by an outsider that it might change is regarded as impertinent.

Yet the AEF is neither a family affair nor an entertainment. Its grip on all the numerous sectors of the engineering industry is strong, but its organisation is weak. The combination is damaging, not just to the union itself, but to the industry and to the economy of which that industry is so integral a part. A study of the AEF is a study in microcosm of much that is wrong with the British trade union movement.

The AEF is the result of a series of amalgamations on a base created by the Amalgamated Society of Engineers, founded in 1852. It is difficult to discover whether non-conformism or craft was the motivating force behind the early development of the union. Certainly craft was important: in the mid-1960s old men could be heard complaining that the union had not been the same since the amalgamations of the early 1920s which brought semi-skilled men into membership. (I actually cross-questioned the man who told me this to make quite sure that he was serious; he was not amused.)

But there is a Biblical streak too. As late as 1960, the union's rule book was prefaced by prose which exhorted the membership to greater things. It spoke of organisation giving men 'a special character . . . it keeps them compact and concentrates their efforts towards one end'. The Kingdom of Heaven seemed never far from their thoughts. But, to be fair, the condition of life on earth predominated, and there were few illusions about that. The same preface states: 'We are ready to admit that, whilst in constant employment, our members may be able to obtain the necessities of life, but there is a fear, and by no means a groundless one, that employment may not be constant. The merest circumstance in the commercial world may influence the condition of thousands of working men; and, when thrown out of employment, all a man's arrangements of a domestic nature are subverted, and his hopes of being enabled by his own frugality to improve his social condition are proved only to be a dream.' Now that is a text for trade unionism during the 1920s and the 1930s; it hardly seems relevant to decades of full-employment, even with its sudden redundancies and post-take-over 'rationalisations'.

Admittedly, the preface disappeared from the latest edition of the rule book, published in 1965, but the thoughts have not been so easily erased. The notion of insecure employment still dominates the men who run the AEF, and, in many cases, it springs from the Marxist conviction that capitalism will destroy itself. Marxism has overtaken Methodism as the strongest single creed in the AEF. The conviction does not exactly smooth relationships with highly pragmatic technocrats in industry, who rarely question the modern mixed economy's assumptions.

The AEF's constitution is not, however, Marxist oriented. On the contrary, it is based on the separation of the powers worked out by the founders of the American nation. There is an Administration, which consists of the President and the seven executive councillors, whose power is limited by the union's 52-man National Committee which meets annually at a seaside resort to decide the policy of the union. The formal purpose of the Administration is to carry out that policy faithfully and unquestioningly.

There is a bureaucracy, headed by the general secretary, whose job it is to serve the executive. There is a Supreme Court, called the final appeal court, manned by lay members of the union, from which all officers, with the exception of the head of the bureaucracy, are rigorously excluded. Finally there are the States. The States in the AEF are the district committees, and the founders of the engineering union were as determined as the authors of the American constitution to protect their autonomy. As in America, one of the greatest running battles in the AEF is between the executive (or Federal power) and the district committees (or States). It is fought with all the vigour of the American States-righters, and it influences the innumerable elections held at all levels of the union. Hugh Scanlon, who became President in 1967 after years of intense political warfare against the right-wing forces led by his predecessor Lord Carron, won partly because he promised to restore the power of the National Committee which had been eroded by Lord Carron's executive.

Exponents of the art of AEF politics proudly describe the system as the most democratic in the world. This, like the reports of Mark Twain's death, is an exaggeration; the union is democratic in the same way that the American constitution was democratic during the 19th century. The AEF still does not grant full citizenship to women or to men who pay less than full dues (they are not allowed to sit on the final appeal court, for instance); and, as in America, the rural areas have more influence than their membership warrants. Each division (a collection of district committees), no matter what its membership, sends two delegates to the National Committee; and each district, even if it has only one branch, is equally represented on the divisional committees.

If the AEF is democratic, it is riddled with the excesses of democracy. But it is doubtful whether it is as democratic as its faithful think. Its politics have been described as Byzantine: a combination of Tammany and the Chinese Warlord system is perhaps more accurate. The effect of political infighting on the day-to-day working of the union is, naturally, quite devastating. Virtually every action is motivated, to a greater or lesser degree, by internal politics. It means that one power group in the union is continually trying to dissipate the strength of another, and so all the groups are weakened. Morale and internal organisation are, to put it delicately, not all they might be.

One of the most striking characteristics is that its leaders often have no knowledge of events which vitally effect the union's operation. The autonomy of district committees means that they only call in the executive when they are in bad trouble, and even then many do so very unwillingly. This can lead to some shockingly embarrassing moments for the leadership. During the Ford strike, in 1969, for example, when the AEF was fighting its battle against 'penalty clauses' as a matter of principle, Mr Scanlon had no idea that earlier a group of AEF members had accepted a much tougher set of clauses at the rolling mill owned by Henry Wiggin in Hereford. Indeed, the company's lawyers had informed the management that, in their opinion, the agreement was legally binding. It made Mr Scanlon's principle look even less convincing than it might otherwise have done.

What had happened in Hereford was that the stewards had reported the agreement to the district committee, as the rules tell them to, and the district committee had sanctioned it. It was none of Mr

Scanlon's business, and since Mr Scanlon is loyal to the constitution, he never complained at the embarrassment. But this means that the acknowledged leaders of the AEF cannot always lead. Even when the executive uses its power to intervene in disputes, the fruits of intervention must be referred back to the district committee concerned before they can be accepted by the men involved. It is a tortuous system, designed to produce maximum rank and file control, which gives no one control. The union is often on the brink of chaos, and the job of an AEF leader rather like that of an advance man taking a company across a minefield.

It also makes it decidedly difficult for the AEF to aid the TUC in its own efforts to resolve troublesome strikes. The autonomy of the districts means that it is, in effect, unconstitutional for the AEF executive to submit a dispute to TUC arbitration, since they cannot be asked whether they agree to a TUC investigating committee's terms for settlement: they would be ordered to accept it. If the district cares to ignore the TUC, there is nothing in the rules to prevent them.

So the job of an AEF leader is trickier than that of any other leader in the trade union movement. He has, to some extent, responsibility without power, but the difficulties are multiplied by another of the constitutional safeguards written into the rule book –a state of almost permanent election. The authors of the rule book decided that the best way to protect the members against slovenly or dictatorial rule was to force the union's officials to submit to re-election with monotonous regularity. The top leadership of the union has to fight for its jobs three years after its first election, and every five years after its second election victory. It is this requirement which has made the union so riven by factional infighting. The *sine qua non* of machine politics is that the members of the machine be continually active, and the AEF penchant for elections means that there is always a campaign in which the two machines–left and right–are able to organise their forces, and display their political dexterity.

The man in position is always looking over his shoulder, and often he can be pushed by militants for whom he has little sympathy because he desperately needs their votes in a forthcoming election. The leadership is less able to sit and think, and virtually unable to get up and tell a group of members that they are behaving foolishly and bringing discredit on the union. Elected officials are scurrying about the country courting favour at a pace which is not only injurious to their health, but their efficiency too. Few trade unionists work harder than the President and the executive members of the AEF. Most trade unionists wonder to what effect their AEF colleagues work so hard.

By 1969 evidence was growing that the members of the union were beginning to tire of the permanent struggle for power. Traditionally, about 10 per cent of the membership was active in the affairs of the union: a small percentage, but a large number (10 per cent is more than 100,000 engineers). By the end of the decade, however, the core was diminishing. District Presidents who could call 40 shop stewards to a meeting a few years earlier, were finding it difficult to get a quorum. Individuals still cared about the activities of their shop stewards on the factory floor negotiating local rates of pay and conditions, but fewer and fewer were attending branch meetings, since membership of AEF branches is based on a man's place of residence, not work. All but the strongest district committees were weakened by the trend, and the weaker the district committees, the greater the problems of national control. Poor communications were becoming even worse. To correct this decline a highly efficient and imaginative organisation was needed to back the leadership. In the 1960s, as in every other decade, the AEF lacked it: the very idea was in conflict with the character of the union. The rank and file, meeting in the National Committee, have always seemed to take positive pleasure in spoiling plans to make the union more efficient. The attitude is illustrated by the salaries the union pays as well as by anything else.

Most British trade unionists (printing workers are an exception) get trade unionism on the cheap, but none get it as cheap as the members of the AEF, whose full membership dues are 3*s*. a week, exactly the same as they were in 1960. Nor is this an accident. A slow smile spreads over the face of a militant member of the union as he tells you that: 'You can't pay the leadership too much or else they'll lose contact with the shop floor.' As if any official of the AEF, under constant pressure of re-election, could ever lose contact with the shop floor. So the President of the union, the second largest in the land, gets a salary of £2,200 a year, as does the general secretary; executive councillors get £1,760; the national organisers £100 a year less, and the full-time district secretaries £1,530 a year. If wages like that were negotiated for members working in the Midland motor factories they would all leave the union the next day. But they expect virtue and frugality from their leaders. It is a mean-minded attitude which, astonishingly, receives some support in the higher reaches of the union, especially from the left-wing. Admittedly, motor workers do not receive expenses on the scale paid to AEF officials, but a man cannot live by expenses alone, nor should he have to do so; and the fringe benefits of a car and a cheap mortgage on a house in London barely improve the basic position.

Meanness towards the men at the top also has its effect on the organisation of the union. This, as we have seen, is the responsibility of the general secretary, now Jim Conway, a man who engages and controls all the staff of the union, and who can be fined 10*s*. if he fails to issue his quarterly report by the 8th day of each quarter. The general secretary is responsible for everything, from the use of paper clips and typing paper to the functioning of the computer. And, sadly, the computer is a superb illustration of the improbability and plain incompetence of the AEF.

A story went the rounds shortly after this computer was installed, that the engineer given the delicate task of operating it had moved into a small, wooden foreman's hut built in the air-conditioned room which housed the computer. Apocryphal though it was, the story is not as unfair as it sounds. The AEF always tries to appoint staff from its own membership; mistrust of outsiders is carried that far. Whatever the job is, it is first advertised in the union Journal, and since the rates for the job cannot be higher than the miserable rates paid to senior officials, this could be just as well.

The result, of course, is that the AEF has never had anything like full value from the computer (which it bought, rather than rented, on the advice of consultants). Its primary function is to correlate branch financial returns, and judging by the reactions of some branch secretaries, this is done little, if at all, better than in the days of clerical labour. The real irony is that when the AEF wants any sophisticated research done, it has to rent time on the electricians' union computer. (Leslie Cannon, the President of the ETU, took the opportunity presented by the need to hire a properly-paid computer chief to get his own salary raised; that would be unthinkable in the AEF.) The failure of the computer experiment at the union's headquarters in Peckham, South London, has also increased the union's mistrust of modern office machinery. By moving one pace forward, the AEF pushed itself two paces back.

The attitude taken towards the computer infects all departments at head office. Because the union refuses to recognise a market rate for skilled functions like heading a research department, or a productivity services division, or even managing an office, these jobs are less well done than they ought to be. (Sometimes the union is lucky with one of its members, but those who are any good do not stay too long.) For a union with assets of around £25 million, employing 700 people, 200 of them full-time officials, whose annual expenditure includes £1 million on pensions, half a million on sickness benefits, and £100,000 on dispute pay in an average year, it really is not good enough. Only the membership of the AEF, which seems to take pride in the incompetence of its administration, could conceivably put up with it.

Proposals for change float about the AEF and are considered during those fleeting moments when full-time officials can sit back and think. But none of the proposals envisage fundamental changes; none of the relationships between various power centres in the union are likely to be altered–in rule at least; circumstances might shift them. Such proposals include increasing the number of full-time officials; increasing their salaries; raising the small sums given to the voluntary branch officials; even increasing the dues.

But any prospect of radical change is negligible as long as changes in rule are discussed and agreed by the lay national committee. It is a profoundly conservative body in which the emphasis is rather on the continuing struggle between left and right, than on the service which the union they represent can give to all its members.

If the actions of some of the AEF shop stewards seem irrational and uncontrollable, it is because they lack any context, or reference to any centrally imposed policy or organisation. And, as the leaders admit, it is not as though engineering workers outside the Midlands earn much more money than many of their colleagues in other unions. As entertainments go, the AEF is a tragi-comedy.

The AEF provides many obvious examples of the faults and weaknesses of British trade unionism (it is significant that many of the examples chosen for this book involve the union), but it is by no means a typical example of trade union organisation. Some of the craft unions are modelled on the AEF, but lack its numerical strength; the other great unions in the country are, however, the general workers' unions for non-craftsmen–the Transport and General, and the General and Municipal, who between them organise one-quarter of the workers affiliated to the TUC.

The GMWU offers an intriguing contrast to the AEF since its leadership is constitutionally powerful, but its rank and file often seems to lack independence, guts even. And one of the main reasons for the lack of militancy is low pay. Militants in the trade union movement are usually found among workers like the engineers whose wage levels are around or above average.

AEF delegates to their national committee wave the fat little red rule book as though it were the thoughts of Chairman Mao. It is difficult to imagine anyone in the GMWU waving the slim buff volume, price twopence, which incorporates their rules. It is, quite unlike the AEF's, a permissive document which allows the leadership to do much as it pleases; permissive, that is, except for its sections dealing with industrial disputes, where it becomes quite tough.

One of the stated objects of the GMWU is 'to endeavour to adjust any difference (between employer and employed) by amicable and conciliatory means'. Rule 27, headed 'Disputes', then proceeds to spell out the way that object is to be achieved: 'In no case shall a cessation of work be threatened or take place without the sanction of the District Committee or the National Executive'; and 'no cessation of work shall take place unless two-thirds of the members belonging to the Branch or body immediately concerned have voted in favour of the adoption of such a course'. It is very alien to the AEF's way of doing things. The only GMWU rule likely to evoke any sympathy from most AEF members is the one forbidding members to speak to the press without the approval of an official body of the union.

While engineering craftsmen believed that they knew best, the core of the GMWU'S membership, in industries like gas and in local government, were willing to believe that the leadership knew best. One of the by-products of this has been a tradition of national negotiation–and local passivity, which is best illustrated by the 200,000 local government workers–the dustmen, gardeners, car park and lavatory attendants, for example–whose national rate ranked 26th among the 130 industries whose wage rates are collected by the Department of Employment and Productivity. Their actual earnings, however, came 128th in the list.

Another of the by-products of local inactivity has been a static membership, which for some years hovered between 750,000 and 800,000. Meanwhile the GMWU was developing a reputation for stifling conformity; it was militantly unmilitant, and its members were losing out badly to locally-based militants in the struggle for higher wages. Two thousand Merseyside Ford workers, for example, tired of what they believed to be the pusillanimity of the union during the Ford strike in 1969, left the union to join the TGWU.

This is a condition in which the GMWU could atrophy, and many of the union's critics (and there are many) claim that it already has. But the leadership, especially Lord Cooper, the general secretary, and David Bassnet, one of the union's industrial negotiators, has used its powers to try to arrest the process. A strong and imaginative research department led by an able recruit from N.W.1. named Giles Radice has been established; so has a productivity services division. The effect of the former has been to initiate a reorganisation into trade groups which will give the union a stronger industrial policy locally, and not just at the headquarters (a converted mansion in the London suburbs which accentuates the differences between the GMWU and the AEF: it has a swimming pool, tennis courts and a small golf course). The productivity services division, established much later, in the summer of 1969, is designed to speed the process of local bargaining, particularly in local government, and reduce the deadening impact of immobile national rates. There is a longer-term purpose too; the GWMU is hoping that reorganisation will make the union more attractive when amalgamations are being discussed, for the leadership believes the best way of substantially expanding the union's static membership is by combining with other unions.

Something else has happened at the GMWU; the exigencies of reorganisation have forced the officials to think about the purpose of a trade union. They have concluded that its strength in the future will be to combine local and factory organisations, primarily responsible for collective bargaining, with an efficient headquarters informing and aiding the local bargainers. 'The days of the national trade union centre are over now', say some officials melodramatically. Although the power of the headquarters officials would be reduced, communications between them and the local bargainers would be improved. Emphasis would be switched from authoritarian control to membership participation.

It could well work–must work, some critics would say, or the union will die on its feet. It will demand the alliance of a strong bureaucracy, which the GMWU has more abundantly than most unions in the country, and a leadership whose strength is not solely derived from the rule book.

The need for change in both AEF and the GMWU is demonstrable, but one of the problems in Britain is that there is no model on which to base the reforms. Should any British trade unionists care to look, though, there is a model abroad. Its strength is based on an alliance between a strong leadership and a virile rank and file, backed by an able and well-financed administration. Its headquarters are in Detroit, Michigan, and it is called the United Automobile, Aerospace and Agricultural Implement Workers of America–the UAW for short.

At various times during its brief history (it was founded in 1936) the UAW has displayed many of the faults endemic in the British Trade union movement. It too was prone to damaging political struggles between left and right; the original leadership appeared to lose contact with the rank and file until the Reuther brothers emerged from the rank and file to take control; and its attitude was 'our members, right or wrong' until proper disciplinary procedures were established in plants which recognised the union (an attack was made on the life of the President, Walter Reuther, allegedly by the Mafia, following the union's decision after the war not to defend any member sacked for gambling on the shop floor).

The strength of the UAW now is that it gets what the members want. Its negotiations for higher wages, better fringe benefits and working conditions are good enough to placate a militant rank and file. The pattern is set by the negotiations, conducted by the most senior officials of the union and headed by Mr Reuther himself, with the Big Three motor companies in Detroit–General Motors, Ford and Chrysler. Mr Reuther and his colleagues not only fight the employers, they have to sell what they get to the members. And the sale is done personally, by Mr Reuther, to the representatives of the members working for each of the three companies, so it is very difficult for the leadership to lose touch with the rank and file, and it gives the leaders a moral authority as well. If the members accept their agreement, they understand that it has been made to be kept.

The moral authority of the leadership is, of course, based on its negotiating ability, and this, in turn, is partially based on the quality of its administration. In the UAW's headquarters in Detroit, the computer is not run by a poorly paid member of the union. It is run by a self-contained department, headed by a $20,000-a-year-plus actuary who understands both the computer and the job. 'I'm not one who believes we will be able to bring the computer to the bargaining table, but it does help us with the facts,' says the man concerned, Howard Young. Nor is the research department confined to a couple of rooms at the back of the building: it has half a floor, a staff of 12, a professional librarian, and, incidentally, shares in every company in which the UAW is recognised, so that any information available to a shareholder is available to the union.

It is an impressive operation, designed to fight the giant motor corporations on equal terms. It is, therefore, not cheap, and the dues paid by UAW members are not low either. They amount to two hours' pay a month, which for a skilled toolmaker in a Detroit motor factory amounts to more than 10*s*. a week. Nor are the union's finances encumbered by the kind of fiddling payments to which, for instance, an AEF subscription entitles a member. The AEF gives a skilled member with 10 years in the union 10*s*. a week unemployment benefit for 18 weeks, and 10*s*. sick pay for 26 weeks, dropping to 5*s*. during the second 26 weeks. The impact of this on family finances in a welfare state which pays wage-related unemployment and sickness benefits, is so negligible as to make the whole scheme ridiculous. But the AEF has yet to relate the effect of social changes of this kind to its own services.

The UAW prefers, rightly, to get the employers to finance unemployment and sickness benefits, and they are not satisfied with payments on the scale paid by the union, or even the Government, in Britain. Fringe benefits are an integral part of the contract, and the negotiation of the contract is what really differentiates the UAW from any British union. Since a British union cannot, by law, make a contract with an employer, the analogy may therefore be thought totally irrelevant. But I believe that they should be able to do so.

The agreement between the Chrysler Corporation and the UAW is a pocket-sized volume of 250 pages. It is given to each employee and it contains everything concerning his wages and his working conditions that he needs to know. It covers a remarkable variety of elements. The wage levels–starting at £1 10*s*. an hour for semi-skilled workers in the assembly plants–are good, but only a beginning. Needs ranging from life insurance to payments for in-patient psychiatric care and university education, are covered by the contract. So is the most important of the fringe benefits, the Supplemental Unemployment Benefit, which gives an employee 95 per cent of his after-tax pay for as much as 52 weeks if he is laid off by Chrysler. It knocks the AEF's 10*s*. a week into a cocked hat.

The contract takes away as well as giving, and the most obvious thing to go is the unofficial strike. There are no lightning strikes in the American motor industry because the contract does not allow them. This does not mean that no strikes take place, but the contract lays down the conditions and the timing of the action. It is not a question of refusing to recognise that grievances exist among workers during the three-year term of a contract: on the contrary, the contract assumes they do exist and contains procedures for settling the whole range of them. Individual grievances cases, for instance, must go through a speedy disputes procedure. If they cannot be settled inside the factory (and 90 per cent are), they then go to independent, binding arbitration.

On a larger scale–in the disputes typical of a motor factory, over the speed of the production line, for instance–over which the appeal system has no authority, procedures are equally well defined. The intention is not to make a strike impossible or illegal, but to make quite sure that both sides know what they are undertaking before it is begun and the contract is voided. There must be 60 days' notice of a strike, and seven full days of negotiation following the notice before the strike actually begins. It is remarkable how a statutory period of negotiation cools ardent passions. Strikes during the contract may be threatened, but they rarely take place.

A complex agreement of this kind obviously demands a sophisticated policing system, and this is provided by the senior shop stewards. They are full-time officials, paid by the company; one for every 225 workers in a plant. And the most interesting thing about the UAW's shop steward system is that the men are formally recognised by the company, and given formal responsibilities on the shop floor where they prowl, waiting for complaints from the members. The stewards are wholly established figures in the industrial relations system because the day-to-day administration of the system depends on them. How different from the working life of our own shop stewards.

The activities of shop stewards in the United States are by no means wholly circumscribed by the terms of the contract. One local official in Detroit explained somewhat conspiratorially how some obnoxious supervisors had been restrained. There was nothing in the contract which permitted this, but by threatening a strike over issues which were permissible, management got the message and calmed their men down. It was much the same as in Britain, except that in Britain the shop stewards are often unrecognised in the collective bargaining system.

Their powers, their presence even, often depends almost wholly on custom and practice, the principle which has supported British industrial relations at plant level for decades. The formal procedures, negotiated at national level in a vast majority of cases, contain what the stewards regard as minimal rights; the rest are worked out privately between themselves and management. The result is that some stewards, unlike their national leaders, have power without responsibility.

Compared with their leaders, the stewards are also a surprisingly little-known quantity. Only after Lord Donovan's Royal Commission undertook a simple research project did a preliminary composite picture begin to emerge, and the conclusions were significant. It is clear that stewards in general do not deserve to be maligned because of the activities of a militant proportion of their number. In one of the Commission's research papers, W. E. J. McCarthy and S. R. Parker conclude that the estimated 175,000 stewards in Britain are, for the most part, a conformist crowd. Of the stewards questioned in the survey undertaken by the Commission, 82 per cent believed that it was preferable to follow the procedure peaceably; only one-fifth supported unqualified strike action. That amounts to a not insignificant total: 35,000 stewards in all.

But the survey also showed that the taste for unofficial action was not always carried into practice: in only 4 per cent of the workplaces investigated had strikes occurred frequently. By revealing this the survey isolated the British problem: local power can occasionally get out of control and be abused. There is, of course, a significant corollary: the greater local power grows, the greater the chances of abuse.

Nor can there be any doubt about the extent of local power after the survey. It demonstrated that 56 per cent of stewards discuss and settle wages 'as standard practice'. An even larger proportion, 73 per cent, deal regularly with working conditions, 49 per cent with hours of work, and 34 per cent with disciplinary procedures. Yet only one in 100 stewards work full-time; the rest devote an average of only six hours a week to their stewards' duties.

The unions tend to rely heavily on the stewards without really recognising their role or their power. As might be expected, the AEF's rule book offers a perfect example of this. The duties of shop stewards are defined in Rule 13, and they are virtually all administrative: to examine and sign contribution cards; to sign up new employees; to see that men are receiving approved rates; and to be the contact between the factory and the district committee.

Constitutionally, that is all. The book states explicitly that a steward may interview a representative of management only when accompanied by another member, and even then an important proviso is added. 'No question involving a principle, change of practice, or stoppage of work shall be determined in any shop until it has been reported to and ratified by the district committee.' In other words, the stewards are not officially trusted to act on their own, though, needless to say, they do.

The rule would be less incomprehensible if the AEF was staffed by enough officials to make regular contact between the shop floor and the district committee an easy business. But the average number of stewards for whom each AEF official is responsible is higher than in any other major union in the country –477, compared to 120 in the even larger Transport and General Workers Union. The officials work harder than their colleagues in other unions, but they simply cannot keep up with the volume of work. The inevitable result is greater uncontrolled power for the AEF's stewards.

McCarthy and Parker concluded their Royal Commission research paper by stating that if contacts between stewards and their officials were to be improved, management would have to help by making access easier. And they added a conclusion which is no less true because it has become a truism: membership dues will have to go up if the unions are to be able to afford the number of officials necessary to improve contact between the shop floor and the union. It is an unexceptionable proposal which nevertheless finds strangely few adherents in the unions. When the GMWU, for instance, decided to raise the dues in 1969 from a minimal 2*s.* a week to 2*s.* 6*d.*, the union's annual policy-making conference accepted the idea grudgingly, and only by a small majority.

The stewards are blamed for many of the excesses of the system, but is this surprising when, in many cases, they are fully recognised by neither the union nor the employer? Formal recognition does not necessarily produce responsibility, but it undoubtedly helps. It hardly seems revolutionary to suggest that formal procedures should incorporate what are now accepted practices, and Dr McCarthy thought it 'extremely significant that in general (shop stewards) do not seek to deny that their influence and status would in some way be advanced by a measure of codification'.

There are people who will resist any change which gives the stewards more influence and status (and they are not all on the management side): they believe the stewards have enough already. But it is a Canute-like attitude, for the power of shop stewards is growing inexorably. The solution is to harness it in the factory, and relate it more closely to the official structure of the union, both of which the UAW have done. But few British unions have begun to grapple seriously with the implications of the movement within a movement which the recent explosion of local bargaining has created.

6

Reformers: False Conclusions

During the second half of the 1960s, as we have seen, some kind of trade union reform seemed to be inevitable, and as it turned out, the reason for the proposed reforms in 1969 was economic. The industrial relations system was considered no aid to a permanent economic recovery. Earlier in the decade this had not been the case. Despite a gradually deteriorating economic situation, it was the relationship between the trade unions and the individual, rather than the unions and the economy, which was the predominant concern of the reformers. Anxiety was caused by the closed shop, which could keep men out of work if they could not, or would not, hold a union card, and by restrictive practices. But opposition to restrictive practices was based largely on the absurdity of many of them, and the pure bloody-mindedness of others.

The Conservative Government flirted with the idea of a Royal Commission inquiry for some years. There is little doubt that men like Iain Macleod and Edward Heath would have welcomed the idea, but their terms as Minister of Labour were too short for them to persuade their colleagues that a Commission was worthwhile. A combination of Mr John Hare (Lord Blakenham) and Harold Macmillan made it virtually certain that no Tory Government would undertake an inquiry in the early 1960s; it was well known that the unions would find the idea offensive, and there was no desire to offend the unions with something as insubstantial-seeming as a Royal Commission. So the Tories concentrated their energies on mildly reformist legislation like the Contracts of Employment Act and the Industrial Training Act. Both had the desired effect and pleased the unions.

A different focus for trade union reform appeared coincidentally, in the form of a draughtsman, who had been employed by BOAC, named Douglas Rookes. Rookes sued three union officials (one named Barnard, hence the title of the famous case, *Rookes* v. *Barnard*) for damages, on the grounds that they had threatened a strike unless he was sacked, and that such a threat was unlawful. It was a complex case, and it cast grave doubts on the legislation which gave the trade unions and their officials their basic immunity from legal action. Rookes won his case in the High Court, lost in the Court of Appeal, and finally won it in the House of Lords, and as the hearings dragged on from year to year, the specific issues involved became the subject of a general debate.

In bald outline, the actions of the draughtsmens' union at BOAC appeared to constitute a gross case of interference in individual liberty. But in their attempt to defend the not altogether hapless Mr Rookes, the House of Lords seemed to reinterpret the Trades Disputes Act, 1906. 'The ordinary strike notice', said one authoritative interpretation of their judgement, 'is a threat to commit a breach of contract and is therefore a threat to commit an illegal act which exposes its maker to the risks of an action for intimidation.' The trade union movement was slow to realise the implications of the House of Lords judgement, but when it did so trade union reform became a live political issue.

At the TUC conference of 1964, just two months before the election, Harold Wilson was rapturously received when he promised a new Trade Disputes Act which would confirm the old freedoms. He was as good as his promise, and the Act was passed in February 1965: but at the same time the Government took a decision less pleasing to the unions. Mr Wilson decided to forget the definition he had given of the work of a Royal Commission–that it would take minutes and waste years–and establish one to survey the whole area of trade union law.

The law was its particular reference, but the Commission, when it got under way later in 1965, concentrated on its secondary role; 'to consider relations between managements and employees and the role of trade unions and employers associations in promoting the interests of their members and in accelerating the social and economic advance of the nation.' The whole spectrum of labour relations was opened up, and the Commission was empowered to investigate every section of it.

The unions were not outraged: they merely considered the whole business rather irrelevant. Once the Government's determination to establish the Commission was clear, so was George Woodcock's determination to have a seat on it and so influence its course from inside. After some weeks badgering Ray Gunter, Minister of Labour, he had his way. To ensure balance, Gunter also appointed Sir George Pollock, from the defunct British Employers Confederation, to represent the employers. The result was that the Commission was polarised from the start. The members who mattered most were the leading spokesmen for two conflicting ideas: one upholding the purely voluntary system of industrial relations unfettered by law, and the other proposing with varying degrees of conviction that a framework of law ought to be imposed on the unions.

Many of the Commissioners became redundant as the proceedings stretched from months into years. The struggle became purely one in which each side tried to grind the other down. When the final report emerged, signed by all the members, it was obvious that victory had gone to Mr Woodcock and his allies. The opposition was in disarray. Five of them signed four addenda, supplementary notes, and notes of reservation, but none of these added up to a minority report. They simply had not been as single-minded as Mr Woodcock and his allies, who also had the advantage of a well-trodden defensive position. They were stoutly defending a situation which had existed for almost 100 years. The rest were trying to suggest ways of changing that condition, and unanimity was difficult, if not impossible. The construction of a new system for industrial relations is a troublesome task, and none of Mr Woodcock's opponents, with the exception of the Director of Studies of the Royal Institute of International Affairs, Andrew Shonfield, took the time to overcome that trouble.

The polarisation of the Commission also prevented either side from establishing a coherent philosophy of trade unionism to run through the report. If it had been able to analyse the purposes of trade unionism it would have been a more convincing document. As it turned out, it was a pedestrian piece of work, but it was a useful one since it provided a starting point from which to continue the debate about trade union reform. This is much less than the Commissioners had hoped for when they began, and their disappointment is understandable. It is a poor epitaph for an ambitious undertaking.

The essence of the Donovan Report was contained in the first paragraph of its summary and conclusions. 'Britain has two systems of industrial relations,' it said. 'One is the formal system embodied in the official institutions. The other is the informal system created by the actual behaviour of trade unions and employers' associations, of managers shop stewards and workers.' This was roughly the way in which Hugh Clegg, one of the Nuffield College school of academics which at that time expertly supported the idea of a voluntary system of industrial relations, had begun a paper which was to provide the foundation of the Commission's report.

None of the Commissioners disagreed with Clegg, although none would have stated the case in such absolute terms. It was an over-simplification, true of the engineering industry, but not of many of the lower paid occupations, such as local Government employment. In their case, the national rate fixed by union negotiators and a representative group of employers is usually what appears in the pay packets at the end of the week. Nor is it true of the electricity supply and contracting industry, where the union, the electricians' and plumbers' (EETU/PTU), exercises an unusual degree of control over the actual wage paid. But it was not unreasonable of the Commission to concentrate on the engineering industry, because it led naturally to the next step in the Commission's argument: that 'the central defect in British industrial relations is the disorder in the factory and workshop relations and pay structures promoted by the conflict between the formal and the informal systems.'

This disorder was illustrated by a series of statistics showing the increase in the number of strikes during the decade 1957 to 1967. By isolating the coal-mining industry, and lumping the rest of the economy together, the report stated that the number of strikes had risen steadily from 635 in 1957 to 1,694 in 1967. The single fact which appeared to influence the Commission more than any other was that 95 per cent of these strikes were unofficial. The problem facing the Commissioners was what to do about it, and at this point they ceased to be as good as their statistics.

Early in the deliberations of the Commission it had been agreed that a new institution was needed to supervise industrial relations. It emerged in the final report as the Industrial Relations Commission, and it was established early in 1969 by the Department of Employment and Productivity as the Commission on Industrial Relations (CIR). The dogfight among the Commissioners concerned the powers of the CIR. The Woodcock/Clegg thesis, reinforced by Professor Kahn Freund's well-argued insistence on the unworkability of labour law, was that the flaw in industrial relations lay in the procedures for settling grievances and disputes. The CIR should, therefore, concentrate on critical studies of collective agreements. 'Procedure agreements', the report stated, 'should be comprehensive in scope and should provide for the rapid and equitable settlement of disputes whether they refer to the interpretation of existing or the making of new agreements.' Since collective bargaining is the best method of conducting industrial relations, the argument continued, the CIR should also have the power to initiate investigations into recognition disputes between employer and union.

The analysis and the conclusions were admirably worked out, but their real strength depended on the quality of the assumption on which they were based. Evidently this was that any failure of the voluntary system could be traced directly to the people who operated it. 'We do not think the shortcomings of our existing industrial relations are due to malice or moral weakness on the part of employers, managers or trade unionists. They are primarily due to widespread ignorance about the most sensible methods of conducting industrial relations, and to the very considerable obstacles to the use of sensible and effective methods contained in our present system of industrial relations.' So the sins were of omission rather than commission: the system was fine, sometimes it just didn't work too well.

It was an optimistic assessment, based on the belief that if everyone were as clear-sighted as the Commission, everything would be for the best in the best of all possible worlds. It also implied that trade union reform should come voluntarily from within the system, and not be imposed from without by Government. This was exactly the conclusion which Mr Woodcock wished the Commission to accept when he persuaded Mr Gunter to make him a part of it.

Not all members of the Commission, nor all the commentators who later wrote about it, were as optimistic as Mr Woodcock. And even the victors were forced to accept a caveat. 'If the reform is largely successful,' this stated, 'so that relations in most companies of any size were carried on within the framework of clear and effective agreements, and yet stoppages in breach of those agreements remained a common occurence, it would be possible to consider enacting some penalty against trade unions or workers responsible for such stoppages (and, of course, against managers and employers where they were responsible).' It was a cautious statement, but it was enough to set the tone of the post-Donovan Commission debate, which was: should or should not the CIR have teeth?

This question should, of course, have been hammered out by the Commission itself. But the forces on the Commission who felt that some form of compulsion was necessary were cowed by the proponents of the voluntary system, whose experience was so much greater than their own. Lord Robens, trade unionist and politician-turned-manager (of the National Coal Board), and Sir George Pollock, tried one tactic: they proposed that unofficial strikers should lose financial benefits gained by length of service when, and if, they were made redundant. It was a very selective financial penalty which briefly appealed to a majority of the Commission's members, but which collapsed under the combined assault of Mr Woodcock, and Professors Clegg and Kahn Freund.

The most effective criticism of the majority's assumptions was not written, however, until a final draft of the report had been circulated among the Commissioners. When they saw it they realised, possibly for the first time, the extent of Mr Woodcock's victory. Lord Tangley wrote a qualification from his sickbed. He wanted the CIR to have powers to deregister (and thus remove legal immunity) from a union if it consistently broke procedure agreements into which it had freely entered. But the most devastating criticism of the report was contained in a Note of Reservation by Andrew Shonfield.

'[The report] barely concerns itself', he began, 'with the long-term problem of accommodating bodies with the kind of concentrated power which is possessed by trade unions to the changing future needs of an advanced industrial society.' Mr Shonfield deliberately made clear his support of the Commission's short-term analysis – that the unions were weak, and unable to control their members – so that he could explore the consequences of that loss of control. 'One has to contemplate a situation in which the typical city dweller has been forced into relying on collective services for things that he is no longer able to provide for himself privately . . . It will become less possible in the circumstances which are unfolding to distinguish, in the sharp traditional style of the English Common Law, between public authority and power, and the "private" power of organisations with collective functions, which control the supply of essential goods and services not obtainable from any alternative source.'

Mr Shonfield pointed out that the Commission had partially recognised this view, and had acted on it. In fact, the action was more an accident than any design. In their discussion of the law and the unions it had become clear that judgement in a case known as *Stratford* v. *Lindley* had seemed to alter the interpretation of the Trades Disputes Act. The judgement stated that a union could be sued for damages when a company had been forced to break contracts because of tortious action by a union which did not appear to be in strict 'furtherance or contemplation of a trade dispute'. The Commission wanted to remove this anomaly, but Lord Donovan demanded a *quid pro quo* from the unions. He decided, and won a

7–5 majority for his proposal, that immunity under the Act should apply only to registered trade unions and employers' associations (a new form of registration was also proposed). The effect of this was to remove immunity given to unofficial strike leaders, who were not acting as representatives of a union, from court actions for damages because they induced workers to break of their contracts of employment.

This was too much for Mr Woodcock and his allies, who opposed it, but it was not enough for Mr Shonfield, who wanted a good deal more. 'I start from the proposition that the deliberate abstention of the law from the activities of mighty subjects tends to diminish the liberty of the ordinary citizen and thus place his welfare at risk,' he wrote. So Mr Shonfield proposed a CIR with judicial powers to intervene in disputes between unions, disputes between employers and unions over recognition, and restrictive practices, but, most important, with the power to investigate areas in which there was 'evidence of serious friction in industrial relations' at will, and without permission from the Secretary of State for Employment and Productivity. The CIR would have powers to order either or both sides in a dispute 'to bargain in good faith', and could impose small monetary fines on parties ignoring its recommendations. He also suggested that the law which prevents unions making binding agreements with employers be changed so that 'the inducement to promise anything' should be strengthened.

Mr Shonfield's hurried Note was hardly a reservation. It actually attacked the basic assumption on which the report was founded and, in effect, rejected the conclusions it reached. But while the report was being hammered out he was isolated. Only when he finally put his thoughts on paper did he receive any support, and by then it was too late to influence the Commission. He did, however, have a considerable influence on those who had to act on the Commission's report. His was undeniably one of the most influential notes of Reservation ever added to the report of a Royal Commission.

While Lord Donovan's Royal Commission was making a stately progress through the field of industrial relations, the Labour

Government was becoming increasingly anxious about the political effects of its delay. By 1967 Ray Gunter was convinced that sweeping reforms were necessary; he actually favoured the legally-binding contract, but if that was not to be acceptable to most of his colleagues, he wanted something which would give him material for legislation. The fact was that in large sections of both parties, Labour and Conservative, a mood was developing which could only be satisfied by legislative reforms, and Labour did not want to have to be seen stealing yet another of the Conservatives' major items of policy. But the Conservative Party not only beat the Government to the post, it beat the Donovan Commission too. The Party's policy document *Fair Deal at Work* was deliberately published two months before the Commission's report. The Party managers had a shrewd idea of the Donovan Report's contents, and knew it would be widely considered a weak and vacillating document, so they decided to bring out their own tough policy in the hope of reducing the Commission's impact. They succeeded.

Donovan's basic assumption was that industrial relations were poor because the unions were weak, and therefore unions should be strengthened. The Conservative policy, on the other hand, was based on the assumption that industrial relations are poor because the unions are strong, and they should therefore be weakened. *Fair Deal at Work* was, however, carefully constructed to please all wings of the Party. The men of goodwill like Robert Carr, who wish to work with rather than against the unions, were the dominant influence, but there was enough in the document to satisfy the union bashers. Nor is this a surprising tactic for the Tory Party; by undermining the trade unions, they could well undermine the organisation of their political opponents, the Labour Party–which is, after all, financed by the trade unions.

The essence of the Tory case is this: 'A fair, relevant and sensible framework of law, while providing no panaceas, can exert stabilising pressures and help to raise general standards in the way men do business together. And we believe the piecemeal, anomalous–and, in some respects, unjust–provisions of our own trade union law tend to handicap rather than help industry in tackling the human problems which inevitably spread from industrial change.'

As it turned out, the Tory programme was designed to curtail the right to strike, and to make the unions pay for what remained of it; the right to sue for damages–granted to trade unions, employers' associations, members of trade unions and members of employers associations–is the most persistent feature of the programme. The Tory alternative withdraws many of the traditional legal immunities granted to the unions; the most important to be repealed being that of section 4 of the Trade Union Act, 1871, which meant agreements between unions and employers would be on the same basis as any commercial contract. (Unless a union could positively persuade an employer that their agreement should not be legally binding.) Cases for breach of contract were to be heard before newly established Industrial Courts; there would be a statutory limit to the damages they could award; and both unions and employers' associations would be able to sue members whose contract-breaking actions had led to an award of damages against them. In case these procedures failed to put a stop to economically damaging strikes, *Fair Deal at Work* also proposed a statutory 60-day cooling off period in strikes which endangered the national interest; this was to be allied to a compulsory ballot among members who were being asked to strike.

Some immunities were to remain, of course, but they would be granted only to unions which complied with the conditions for registration imposed by a new registrar who would survey union rules and decide whether its membership was 'substantial' enough: even then the definition of a trade dispute during which the immunity held good was considerably narrowed. It excluded the following varieties of strike: sympathetic strikes, and blacking the goods and services of an employer not directly involved in a dispute with his employees; inter-union disputes; strikes to enforce the closed shop; and strikes to prevent an employer hiring labour unacceptable to the union.

These proposals do not form just a marginal incursion into the trade unions' right to strike. (Had the law been operative in 1968,

223 of the 2,378 stoppages in all industries and services registered by the DEP would have been conducted without the benefit of legal immunity: 51,900 workers were involved in these strikes, which led to the loss of 444,000 working days, just under 10 per cent of the total lost during the year.) The *quid pro quo* offered – of compulsory recognition in some circumstances – was hardly substantial enough to appease the unions: for it was balanced by the proposed removal of the right to organise a closed shop, in which workers cannot get work unless they have a union card. The Tories offered to accept the union shop, in which it is compulsory for a man to join the union after he has been hired, but even then safeguards were built into the system: a man's dues need not be paid to the union, they could go to a charity of his choice.

These proposals were harsher than Tory spokesmen would admit in their public affirmations of the policy, which concentrated on legally binding contracts more than any other single item. Even so, the plans in *Fair Deal at Work* provoked surprisingly little response from the trade unions. They seemed to believe that they could afford to ignore the Conservative Party's policies for industrial relations. There was, apparently, a faith that something would turn up to prevent incursions by the law, and the Donovan Report, when it appeared in June 1968, must have looked remarkably like divine intercession. The unions must have thought that the report would set the pattern for the lifetime of the Labour Government; that, though the clamour for fundamental trade union reform was growing, Donovan had relieved the pressure.

But the Donovan Report had the opposite effect. It was so mild and so optimistic that its publication actually intensified the demand for reform. The first reaction to the Report inside the Department of Employment and Productivity was disappointment. Its senior officials had hoped for some proposals which would allow them to intervene more directly in a state of industrial relations which many of them thought rotten. But shortly after the Royal Commission's report appeared the Ministry of Labour had gained its new name and a new Minister.

The Government, determined to recognise the growing power of the old Ministry with a new title, decided that the new powers needed a powerful Minister. Barbara Castle, who had been a startling success at the Ministry of Transport, was transferred to St. James's Square, and given the title of First Secretary of State. The DEP now had the seniority to introduce sweeping reform, and the arrival of Mrs Castle unquestionably stiffened its will to do so. She is a socialist interventionist. Put simply, she believes that she knows what is good for people, even if they do not. Within months at the Department, she became known as 'the Tudor Monarch', and with her flaming red hair, her autocratic temper, and her determination to alter the whole direction of British industrial relations, it was an apt title.

Yet the full force of Mrs Castle's own will was not really applied to the problem until the middle of November 1968. Her reformist zeal was not aroused by the drafts of the post-Donovan White Paper which began to circulate in her own Ministry in the autumn, but her mind was made up during a November week-end spent at a Civil Service staff college in Sunningdale. It was an interesting 48 hours, and it concentrated Mrs Castle's mind admirably.

The first half of the week-end–Friday night and Saturday morning–was spent by Mrs Castle and her senior officials in conference with selected trade unionists and employers. The experience seems to have been almost cathartic for Mrs Castle. The Trade unionists, led by Mr Woodcock, were simply not interested in proposing any new formulae for dealing with the problems of industrial relations. They asked insistently: what did the Government propose to do? When they knew that, they said, they would react and tell the Government what they thought of their plans. Mrs Castle, appalled by so passive an attitude, concluded that if that was what they wanted she would give it to them. On the Sunday she and her officials, working alone, decided on the first draft of the Government's White Paper, which was to be called *In Place of Strife*, and it went a good deal further than the Donovan Report did.

When the White Paper appeared in January, it presented an indictment of Britain's industrial relations. 'Our present system,' it said, 'has substantial achievements to its credit, but it also has serious defects. It has failed to prevent injustice, disruption of work, and inefficient use of manpower. It perpetuates the existence of groups of employees, who, as a result of the weakness of their bargaining position, fall behind in the struggle to obtain their full share of the benefits of an advanced industrial economy. In other cases management and employers are able unfairly to exploit the consumer and endanger economic prosperity. There are still areas of industry without any machinery for collective bargaining at all.'

The White Paper concluded that in general unions are weak, and need strengthening, just as Donovan did, but it added a touch of Shonfield to Donovan's interpretation by superimposing the view that in certain groups of union members are too strong, and their power should be curbed.

The result was what became known as 'the penal clauses'. The Minister was to take the power to impose a 28-day cooling-off period in unofficial or unconstitutional (official but in breach of agreed procedure) strikes; a ballot could be ordered to precede an official strike, which could then not take place if the members voted against it; and unions failing to adhere to a Ministerial order to end an inter-union dispute could be fined. The penalties to be levied on individual strikers who ignored a Government return-to-work order were never actually defined (they would have been in the region of £20 to £25), but the White Paper clearly revealed a new attitude to industrial relations: workers and trade unions were to take limited legal responsibility for some of their actions; and the DEP was to be given positive powers to intervene in strikes–like the Girling and Ford disputes–which endangered the national economy.

The White Paper was, in fact, an unsatisfactory amalgam of the Donovan Report and *Fair Deal at Work*; neither one nor the other. Most of the recommendations were pure Donovan: a CIR without teeth, registration of agreements, compulsory recognition where a majority of workers wanted it, safeguards against unfair dismissal, and various other such proposals which would aid efficient and ambitious trade union officials. But the sting was in the tail, and the tail was the adoption in principle of the Tory proposals for a cooling-off period and strike ballots.

But there was a difference between the DEP and the Conservative's proposals, and it reflected Mrs Castle's somewhat arrogant faith in her own good will. The Conservatives suggested that there should be a buffer between a Minister and his or her actions, with the Minister asking the Industrial Court for an injunction to cool off a strike or impose a ballot. There was no such buffer in 'In Place of Strife'. The most objectionable thing about the White Paper was not the penal clauses which caused so apocalyptic a battle between the Government and TUC later in the year, it was the power it gave to a Minister and his or her officials.

It was not surprising that Barbara Castle and the senior officials at the DEP should invest themselves with such powers. Neither she nor a majority of her senior officials really needed much prodding. But the proposals went further than even their admirers thought justified. In effect, the only sanction which could have been brought to bear on the First Secretary and her Department was a vote of confidence in the House of Commons, which is rare. The powers were even carried to the extent of allowing the DEP to write the motion which would go on the pre-strike ballot: the implication was that the unions themselves could not be trusted to do so. It was interesting that the first proposal which angered the TUC when they heard of it was this one. It carried the notion of intervention too far.

The idea of a strike ballot was dropped when the Government decided shortly after the Ford strike, in April 1969, to introduce a short Bill which would contain all the other penal clauses and a few sweeteners for the unions, like compulsory recognition of trade union membership, and the prevention of Friendly Societies from having rules which debarred members from belonging to a trade union. It also established the CIR as a statutory body (it had already been given a *de facto* existence shortly after publication of the White Paper).

The trade unions had, however, decided some three or four months before the announcement of the short Bill that it was not only the strike ballot which upset them. All the penal clauses did, particularly the one which gave the Minister the right to intervene and 'cool off' a strike for 28 days. But there was no apparent opposition to one of the most significant recommendations in the White Paper: the one which enabled the CIR to recommend, and the Secretary of State to order (to quote the White Paper) the 'exclusion of one or more unions from recognition, with penalties for breach of the order by either the employer or a union'. It meant that only one of a series of unions competing for membership would be recognised, and it was the first approach to the American principle of the single bargaining agent in which one union, rather than a multiplicity of unions, has bargaining rights in a factory.

The events of the two months of May and June reflected credit on few of the groups involved. Trade unionists talked of an attack on their 'liberties', which were hardly at stake–the attack, if anything, being on the irresponsibility of a few of their members. But the movement, sensing that a principle was involved, decided on an all-out fight; and to the great surprise of most people, they won it. The Government, having spoken of the Bill as an essential part of their strategy for economic recovery, dropped it on 18 June.

It was as tense and dramatic an occasion as the 1906 debates, although, this time, the warfare was conducted outside the Chamber of the House of Commons; and the victory was won–as in 1906–by the backbench members of the Parliamentary Labour Party (incited, admittedly, by the trade union movement to which many of them belonged). The Prime Minister had insisted privately and stated publicly that he was determined to put the national interest above sectional interests, but members of his own Party prevented him from doing so.

There was no single motive for their rejection of the Bill: some of the Government's opponents on the left opposed it because they denied the right of the Labour Party to interfere with the organisations which gave it its birthright, and which still financed and manned the Party machine. Others simply did not like the Bill, particularly the powers it invested in Mrs Castle's Department. A smaller group just did not like Mr Wilson, and were happy to adopt any course which would embarrass him; and there were those who did what the unions which sponsored them told them to do. (Nor did it help when one of the junior Ministers in Mrs Castle's Ministry deliberately chose to tell his Parliamentary friends and allies that the Bill was a hopeless mishmash unworthy of the political effort.)

This incongruous coalition was large enough to persuade a majority of Mr Wilson's Cabinet that sectional interests were, after all, rather more important than his conception of the national interest. From that moment on the TUC's victory was inevitable: all that remained was for the Prime Minister and Mrs Castle to salvage as much as they could from the wreckage of their policies, and put as good a gloss on the settlement as they could.

The proposed Bill was not, of course, essential to the economic recovery, it was a tentatative step in the direction of trade union reform, and as such it was valuable. Once positive legislation has been passed by Parliament it does not remain static on the statute books. Trade union law is dynamic, and there is little doubt that the Industrial Relations Bill, 1969, which never left the office of the Parliamentary draftsman, would have been just the first of a series of Industrial Relations Bills.

Nevertheless, the surrender by the Government to the TUC was conditional. If the TUC were to have their way over the penal clauses, they must offer something in return, said the Prime Minister, and although he did not get as much as he wanted, the TUC's *Programme for Action* was a step in the right direction. 'The Government has greatly exaggerated the effects that stoppages of work have on the British economy,' it stated . . . 'Nevertheless, the general council accept that every effort should be made to reduce the number of stoppages of work and also recognise that for the most part disputes are symptoms of underlying deficiencies in industrial relations that in some industries may well impede Britain's economic advance in more significant ways.' After that opening the general council and the trade union movement was dragooned into accepting something which Mr Woodcock had fought for unsuccessfully throughout the decade: more power for the TUC.

It was given grudgingly, on the insistence of the Government, but in one respect at least, it was real. There was always a chance that the Government's legislation would push the TUC into taking a more positive role in inter-union disputes, and the new role did emerge in *Programme for Action*. Affiliated unions were obliged to report disputes among their own members, and submit themselves and their opponents to binding arbitration by fellow trade unionists chosen by the TUC. It had always seemed to be the most sensible way of dealing with disputes of this kind.

But what concerned the Government more was unofficial and unconstitutional strikes. The first draft of *Programme for Action* offered only crumbs of comfort there, and the Prime Minister and Mrs Castle spent many hours trying to force the general council to concede something more substantial. In the end the TUC agreed to apply to unofficial strikes the method used for settling disputes between unions about membership–the Bridlington procedures. Committees of trade unionists were to hear the case of a union whose members were on strike, and advise it on tactics and action.

It was an advance on anything the TUC had been willing to offer when its special Congress met in Croydon early in June 1969, but the scepticism which greeted the compromise when it was announced by Harold Wilson was hardly surprising. Not only had the TUC failed to display the will to increase its powers earlier in the decade, but the proposed formula was open to cynical manipulation. It would not be surprising if, in some classic unofficial (and, indeed, official) strikes a committee of trade unionists did not turn a blind eye to the dubious tactics of one of their colleagues, and suggest a settlement totally unacceptable to the employer involved. Settling unofficial strikes is different in virtually every significant way from settling membership disputes. There is an employer involved for a start, who might not be so amenable to TUC intervention.

At the end of a period in which trade union reform had become inevitable, the TUC's concessions were a decidedly cautious start, and they found noticeably little support from the other side of the industrial relations conflict, the employers themselves. It hardly reflected a consensus of the interested parties; on the contrary, it was a rather shoddy deal between two wings of the Labour movement.

7

Abroad: Experience Ignored

When the Australian trade union leader, Clarie O'Shea, was sent to jail for contempt of court in the spring of 1969, the incident confirmed all the prejudices of the British trade unions. They believed it demonstrated conclusively that once the law was brought into industrial relations the bailiff and the jailer might just as well be present at the negotiating table, since they would be such central figures in all industrial disputes.

The attitude was based on ignorant exaggeration of the Australian law. Indeed, some Australian trade union leaders actually claimed that one way to overcome their problem was to introduce legislation similar to the Bill which Barbara Castle was hawking round Britain at the time. They were particularly intrigued by the 28-day cooling off period, which they thought would be a pleasant change from compulsory arbitration. The Australian case, however, was just another excuse for a display of the British trade union movement's xenophobia. They believe things are better ordered at home, and their attitude to less experienced trade union movements overseas has always been slightly patronising.

Nor is the prejudice confined to the trade union movement. Lord Donovan's Royal Comission seemed to regard foreign experience of industrial relations as largely irrelevant. Only two foreign countries, the United States and Sweden, are mentioned in the index, and in the body of the report their attempts to impose a framework of law on the unions are treated with scant respect. The Swedish 'peace obligation' during the term of a contract between employer and union is described and dismissed: it did not conform to the Commission's own analysis. The Taft–Hartley Act, passed by the United States Congress in 1947, is given even less consideration.

There was just one aspect of American labour relations which seemed to tempt the Commissioners: 'In the United States and Canada where collective contracts lasting for a fixed period are negotiated in the light of the prosperity of the individual company and where therefore during the currency of the contract employees have the incentive to accept change derived from the knowledge that the more efficient the company becomes the higher the wages it will be able to afford when a new contract comes to be negotiated . . .' the report said tortuously. It went on rather sadly: 'In this country the system does not provide any formal method of linking levels of pay with the efficiency of companies, with the result that workers are encouraged to wrest what increases they can piecemeal as opportunities arise. The introduction of new methods or machines offers such opportunities. Thus change itself becomes the subject of dispute and controversy, and is too often as a result delayed, or not even attempted.' It would be reasonable to suppose, on the basis of this comment, that the Commission would look sympathetically on a system which embraced 'company collective contracts.' Not at all; they did not even recommend that a contract should be legally binding if both parties wished it to be. The suggestion was too much at variance with their fundamental objection to any legal intervention in industrial relations.

While Donovan was busy defending the essentially voluntary system in Britain, however, various pressure groups which opposed the Commission's analysis had begun to seek inspiration abroad. The process was part of the increasingly rapid erosion of the idea that British industrial relations were the best in the world. The more the system was attacked, the more experience overseas seemed relevant. In *Fair Deal at Work*, the Conservative Party did not so much look abroad, as use events abroad to justify their own decision to impose a rigorous legal framework.

But the document did correctly analyse the fundamental differences between the British system, and others. Foreign collective agreements, it pointed out, are enforceable in the courts – methods vary but the principle is universal. Trade unions and employers' association are corporate bodies answerable in the courts for their actions, and for the actions of their servants and agents. Further, in most countries the right to collective bargaining and to strike (and, of course, lock out) is explicit in the law. But the rights are often circumscribed, and the Tory document went on with some glee to describe the limitations on the right to strike in America, Canada, Australia, New Zealand, Japan, Germany and other western European countries. 'A feature common to the history of most countries has been the initial resistance by trade unions to comprehensive legislation,' *Fair Deal at Work* went on, 'yet once passed these laws have come to be accepted; and the legal sanction as a measure of last resort has generally proved to be a help, not a handicap, to responsible union activity.'

Whether or not this makes a legislative package more palatable to the unions, it is true, and it was one of the factors which persuaded the Department of Employment and Productivity to push ahead with its legislation in the summer of 1969 instead of waiting until the winter. Had the Labour Cabinet not cut the process short it would have become an increasingly popular justification of the decision to reform in spite of the opposition of the trade unions.

The DEP had already filched, and bowdlerised, some policies for its Bill from abroad. The cooling-off period had its origins in Swedish and American legislation; intervention in demarcation and recognition disputes is a part of the responsibilities of the American National Labour Relations Board, to which the CIR also bears some fleeting resemblances. For reasons of pride, the DEP has always been loath to admit that it was influenced by Government policies in other nations, but it is true nonetheless, and there is no reason why they should not have been.

Once the Government began to look enviously at nations in which a balance of payments crisis was not endemic, it was bound to start looking at the way they conducted their industrial relations – a healthy departure which broadened the self-absorbed context in which the problem had always been discussed in Britain. So what is worth looking at?

To start with the least relevant – the trade unionists who used Australia as a bitter example of the terrors of legislation had a point.

There the legal framework has been drawn so tight that the law has strangled the creativity of the trade union movement. Australian law is based on the simple assumption that the object of a system of industrial relations is not only to settle disputes as quickly as possible, but that the two parties to the dispute cannot be trusted to perform the task themselves. The outcome is compulsory arbitration, the effect of which is to squeeze the life out of collective bargaining, with both sides simply offering an extreme case to the arbitration court and hoping for the best.

When arbitration is compulsory the right to strike is, in theory at least, seriously circumscribed. It also tends to give Governments ideas rather above their station. For instance, Australian arbitration authorities have refused to register agreements they consider to be inflationary and against the public interest. This is one way of imposing an incomes policy but it does seem to cut corners more sharply than Governments ought. So the Australian system appears either to emasculate the unions, or to drive their membership to extremes. One would have thought that, in a country so close to China, Mao-ist doctrines might be even less attractive than they seem on the other side of the world. On the contrary, influential sections of the Australian trade union movement have been infected by them.

The study of Germany's example ought, perhaps, to be more profitable. After all, the country lost incredibly few working days through strikes in 1968. The figure was 25,000 compared with over 4 million in Britain; so strikes are not a problem at all. The German system of trade unionism, like so many of its institutions, was imposed by its allies after the Second World War, who imported trade unionists from Britain and America to work it out: and the system they built presumably bore some relationship to their ideal. It was neat and tidy, and full of limitations. The trade unions are politically circumscribed, for example, by the refusal to allow them to strike on issues not directly connected with labour-management relations; and they may not interfere with essential deliveries and services either.

But the great triumph of the German system is its industrial unionism. Sixteen unions organise the eight million members of the German TUC, the DGB, so organisation is not only centralised nationally, it is also concentrated in a few powerful unions. Negotiation is simplified because competition among unions which have similar membership is non-existent. Demarcation disputes can hardly break out when all the workers on a shop floor belong to the same union. It is an ideal system, but one that cannot be imposed on a sprawling trade union movement like Britain's, unless a draconian solution like one proposed by Lord Robens during the Donovan Commission's private hearings is imposed. (He suggested that only unions with more than 40,000 members be registered as trade unions. Even the supporters of industrial trade unionism considered that too dictatorial a method of achieving a worthy end.)

It is a strange and admirable thing that the men who created the German trade union movement after the war should have imposed a system which so exactly suited German industry. It was regimented and disciplined; it demanded responsible behaviour, and got it. Without the system, the German economic miracle might not have been quite so miraculous. Yet it now seems possible that the system was based on too narrow a reading of the German character. The system of centralisation has come under increasingly bitter attack; more local autonomy is being demanded, and must eventually be given. This trend is certainly relevant to Britain; but little else could be profitably transferred.

In 1962, a TUC delegation went to Sweden to see if there was anything to learn, and concluded that, in principle, there was not. The conclusion disappointed many commentators when it was revealed shortly after the delegation's return, but it was not surprising. The Swedes also have industrial unions, and an even more concentrated and co-ordinated national collective bargaining system than the Germans. It is a delicately balanced scheme, perfectly suited to a small, integrated and planned economy (though it did come under considerable strain in the late 1960s). But it does have features which have general application.

Some disputes, over working conditions in the engineering industry, for instance, can be referred to a Labour Court, and the emphasis in this judicial procedure is very firmly on speed. Disputes must be negotiated within two weeks at local level, and within three weeks a local breakdown must be discussed at national level; further disagreement is solved either by independent arbitration or by the Labour Court. Summing up the procedure T. L. Johnston, in his book *Collective Bargaining in Sweden*, says; 'the machinery for settling justiciable disputes is comprehensive, covering both private and public employment, it is swift, and it is peaceful'.

But the principle of independent arbitration is not confined to justiciable disputes; it is also used to solve thorny problems arising from the annual round of wage negotiations. Arbiters can be brought in when thc two sides are stuck at some point during the wage talks, and a second wave of arbitration can be imposed at what appears to the Government to be a critical stage in the talks. It may then appoint a mediation commission. The centralised system of wage bargaining, in which all unions put forward a claim at much the same time, has other attractive side-effects. Mr Johnston makes the point that: 'There has been a tendency for the institutional pressure groups to seek an advantageous place in the income queue, which has in turn led to the idea of equity in income distribution becoming very marked. Such equity is explicit policy only in the case of farmers, but it has gained wide acceptance in an informal way.' Acceptance of any similar principle, in either a formal or an informal way, has been significantly absent from the British system.

It is not surprising that the TUC did not find Swedish practice attractive because it clashed with many of their dearest principles. An element of voluntary action has been removed from the Swedish system, and that, in itself, is enough to condemn it. (Although the TUC might not object to another element of self-imposed compulsion in Sweden: newspapers have grudgingly agreed not to write about the first exploratory stage of national wage talks in which tentative proposals and counter-proposals are made.) Because the TUC does not like the Swedish system, however, it does not mean that Britain has nothing to learn from it.

The combination of speed and peace in the settlement of disputes is an admirable thing, and it is very possible that the peace is a function of the speed.

Speed is often absent from the American style of collective bargaining, which can be as formal as a chess game with as many rules. Some disputes can even go for final settlement to the Supreme Court, the highest in the land. Nevertheless the American experience is probably the most relevant to Britain. Its trade union movement developed later than in Britain and the process was characteristically more violent and corrupt, but its objectives are much the same; and although the legal system differs in many respects, it is based on the English tradition.

What America shows is that unions can work within a framework of the law without being emasculated; it has the best and the worst in the world, and the worst, which are prejudiced and/or corrupt, are not that way because of the law. The purpose of American labour law is twofold: to protect men who wish to join a union from unscrupulous employers (there is an element of protection for employers from unscrupulous trade unions too), and to protect the public generally from the worst excesses on the unions.

The law is based on two Acts of Congress. First the Wagner Act, passed during the ferment of New Deal legislation in 1935, which made it 'illegal for an employer to refuse to bargain in good faith about wages, hours, and conditions of employment with the representative of the employees in a unit for collective bargaining'. It triggered off the great explosion of trade union growth in the United States, and was, in effect, the unions' Magna Carta. Twelve years later a second law was passed by Congress, named the Taft–Hartley Act, designed to redress the balance of power. It introduced the 90-day cooling off period, and ballots in strikes which are classed as 'national emergencies', and it has worked with varying degrees of success ever since–though its failures have almost always been confined to disputes on the docks. Taft–Hartley also attempted to stultify the growth of the unions through a complex legal procedure known as the right-to-work law, and it did succeed in slowing down the growth rate, but good unions, like the

United Automobile Workers, have not been seriously stricken by it.

After the great British debate in the summer of 1969, the cooling off powers in Taft–Hartley is probably the best known provision in American labour law, but it is hardly the most important. The most interesting element in the American system is 'the contract' freely negotiated by union and employer, but legally binding while it is in operation. It does not weaken collective bargaining; on the contrary it results in highly sophisticated bargaining. Nor does it remove the right to strike. (Compulsory arbitration has often been proposed by sections of the Republican Party, it has always been successfully resisted.) The substantial part of the nation's labour law is designed to aid collective bargaining, and contract-making. The legal instrument chosen to assist the process was created by the Wagner Act, and called the National Labour Relations Board.

The NLRB has its headquarters in Pennsylvania Avenue, just down the road from the White House in Washington, but it is independent of the Administration and Congress. Despite the chairmanship being a political appointment, its traditions have remained liberal since it was established during the first Roosevelt Administration. In January 1969 the head of the Board was a gentle Scots-American named Frank McCulloch, and he explained the reason for the Board's existence as follows: 'It is essential in a situation in which there is continued resistance to worker interests. For myself I find it very difficult to understand the resistance. But lawyers have very sophisticated techniques, and they have perfected the techniques of keeping the unions out.'

Mr McCulloch went on to state with evident pride that the NLRB is primarily a mediation body, and only secondarily a law enforcement agency. Large charts are scattered about his office showing the incidence of peaceful settlement of disputes over recognition, or between unions about representation. Of the 17,000 cases brought before the Board in 1968, 90 per cent were settled before it was forced to make a binding decision on the case; in 5·6 per cent of the cases the Board had to make an order; only 5·4 per cent of the cases went to litigation (either party has the right to appeal in the court of appeals against a Board order).

At this final stage wheels begin to grind more slowly. The speed at which the few litigated disputes are settled depends on the amount of work before the courts, and as in most courts everywhere, the American courts of appeal are swamped. 'One of our principal problems is delay,' says Mr McCulloch.

The Board's most useful function, however, is to reduce the tensions which are an inevitable corollary of collective bargaining. There is no better instance of this than the Board's procedures for overseeing the recognition of unions. Once a union can show that 30 per cent of the workers in a factory are interested in recognition, the Board can order that a ballot be held; if more than 50 per cent of the workers vote for the union, then the employer must bargain with it 'in good faith'. The procedure also contains a built-in incentive towards industrial unionism, for the law states that only one union shall be recognised in a single factory or bargaining unit. In 85 per cent of the cases, admittedly, only one union applies for recognition, but in the other 15 per cent the ballot is used to decide which of the competing unions will be recognised.

The procedure has not eradicated demarcation disputes from American industry by any means, but it has reduced their impact, and there is no doubt that it has helped boost union membership. In the last six months of 1968 3,834 ballots were conducted under its auspices; the unions won in 3,416 of them and membership increased by a total of 278,420.

Once an American union is recognised, both sides must make a contract, and most disputes occur at the end of the contract, so the Wagner Act also imposes guidelines to contain these disputes. There must be 60 days' notice of termination in writing; there must be negotiations during that period, and when half the period has passed without a new agreement being made, the Federal Mediation and Conciliation service must be informed. If the union strikes during the 60-day period, the workers lose the protection from dismissal which the Act gives to them.

Protection from dismissal is, in fact, the major immunity granted to American workers by the law. A strike which, for instance, violates a no-strike clause in a contract gives the employer the right to sack or discipline the strikers, but the Wagner Act carefully states the principle that: 'Nothing . . . shall be construed so as either to interfere with or impede or diminish in any way the right to strike.' It merely says that if workers, having agreed not to strike, break the agreement, they must look after themselves. It does not seem to be an unreasonable exercise in law. In fact, few things in the canon of American labour law seem unreasonable. The unions themselves object mainly to the right-to-work laws, and sections of the law which limit their right to picket factories or sites which are strike-bound. For the rest, they have not only learned to live with it, they have learned to gain by it.

Naturally, the American system of labour law has created a lucrative new field for lawyers; 800 are employed by the National Labour Relations Board alone. But it has also broken down the unions' distrust of lawyers; they hire some of the best themselves. Indeed, some of the most engaging and committed people in the American trade union movement are the union lawyers. They are more detached from the scene than front line negotiators, and their advice can be valuable to the men who are trying to wrest money from the employers. Certainly the most valuable lesson to be learned in America is that law does not necessarily hamstring a union movement; it does not necessarily erode trade union liberties; and it does not necessarily quash collective bargaining between the two sides of industry.

One other international experience is worth alluding to here. It has been felt only in Europe, and then only recently, and it is not easy to describe or to explain. It was most easily sensed in Paris during the May revolt in 1968, and it can facilely be described as worker participation in industry.

In Germany after the war, workers in the iron and steel, and coal industry had seats on the Boards; in other industries the employer was forced to accept an elected works council, with access to information, and the right to discuss the policies of the firm. But the idea never really spread. It lay dormant in the rest of Europe until the end of the 1960s, when it suddenly emerged in an inchoate, intangible form. The most articulate French workers suddenly started to complain about the soullessness of industry during the May revolt. Admittedly, they had more time to think about it than they normally do, since the strike was protracted and solidly national. But it was clear that they were gripped by the idea that industrial relations simply have not kept pace with technological change. Men and women spend as much as a third of their adult lives at work, yet they have no significant influence over the environment in which they work. With technological change especially, work becomes less and less creative, and so job satisfaction suffers. The only innovation which might counter this trend (for men will not use fewer machines in the future) is to give workers more responsibility for what they produce, and for the way in which it is produced.

This idea cannot be translated easily into legislative terminology, although General de Gaulle did try. The old visionary somehow grasped the reason for the frustrations and the impatience of many French workers, but the measures he proposed did little more than force French employers to recognise the pathetically weak French trade union movement. It is not really surprising that nothing more tangible than higher wages followed the tumult of the French revolt, but societies which ignore the frustrations of their workers at work do so at their peril. The problem created by the monotony and noise of a production line in a motor factory or the furnaces and rolling mills in the steel industry, for instance, is not easy to solve. But one thing seems certain: higher wages alone are not necessarily enough.

It is difficult for a curious observer to travel and not to be influenced by the institutions and systems, but British trade unions appear to have done just this. It is not that the leaders of the British unions do not travel; on the contrary, some seem to spend an excessive amount of time out of the country. But their curiosity is very rarely aroused. No overseas country has discovered an ideal system which could be adopted wholesale in Britain, because none has the same historical and social experience as Britain. But the British have gone to the other extreme, and seem to believe there is nothing to be learned. It has been thought somehow humbling to have to look elsewhere for new ideas, and this alone has been a brake on imaginative and creative thought. One side-effect is that reformers who do adopt ideas from other countries tend to be stealthy about it. The suspicion grows that they are conspiring to foist nasty foreign policies on an unsuspecting working class. Sadly, it makes necessary reform even more difficult.

8

Proposals: A Framework of Law

The difficulties involved in proposing trade union reform are intimidating. The unions themselves display paranoia at the merest suggestion that all is not well with them, and the prospect of undertaking any radical reforms appears infinitely depressing, for nothing can be done without minimal union co-operation. So flushed were they with their victory over the Labour Government in June 1969 that the unions' belief in their divine right to immunity was actually strengthened. But within six weeks of the announcement of the solemn agreement by which the TUC was pledged to reform itself, a group of strikers demonstrated their own belief in their immunity not only from legislation, but from the intervention of the TUC as well.

It was abundantly clear to anyone who talked to the blastfurnacemen whose unofficial strike halted production at Britain's largest steel mill in Port Talbot, South Wales, in July and August, they they simply rejected all the proposed schemes to deal with strikes. If the Government had won its legislative powers to suspend the strike for 28 days, they would have been ignored. Writs would have been served, and the blastfurnacemen would have taken a perverse pleasure in their court appearances, even if that pleasure might have been alloyed for some by the eventual appearance of bailiffs at their doors. In such circumstances, the probability of the Conservative Party's proposals having any effect would be slim indeed; if the agreement between the blastfurnacemen and the Steel Company of Wales Division of the British Steel Corporation had suddenly been made binding, its shortcomings would immediately have been exposed. The TUC's proposal for ending the blastfurnacemen's strike was eminently reasonable (it was even too reasonable to suit the industry and the Government), but the strikers stubbornly rejected it at meeting after meeting, and the management was just as intractable.

The affair provoked an acute sense of despair: how were such men to be handled? If one looked to distinguished academics for a solution, the despair was magnified. As the blastfurnacemen's strike began, an absorbing paper by two Oxford lecturers Allan Flanders and Alan Fox (Mr Flanders is a member of the Commission on Industrial Relations) was published in the July 1969 issue of the *British Journal of Industrial Relations*. The two accurately describe the breakdown of British industrial relations by invoking the work of 'the father of sociology', the Frenchman Emile Durkheim. Durkheim argued that a stable society was cemented by a series of commonly accepted norms, and that a breakdown or social regulation resulted in a state of normlessness, or *anomie*.

'Our contention', the two authors write,' is that the present state of industrial relations in Britain is better characterised as a proliferation of unrelated normative systems, each resting on only a small area of agreement, in place of more closely integrated systems covering much larger areas, and that the overall effect is equivalent to a progressive breakdown in social regulation.' They add gloomily that there is only a limited appreciation of the urgency and seriousness of the case for reform.

Yet the normative role adopted by Mr Flanders and Mr Fox is as a pair of Cassandras, for they never conclude their argument. They explain the faults of the system, but they do not say how order can be restored. They imply that unless the two sides of industry pull themselves together and work the traditional voluntary system much more successfully than of late, then someone else will have to intervene and do it for them. It is a weak conclusion to a devastating analysis.

The first seven chapters of this book reach the same conclusions as Mr Flanders and Mr Fox: that industrial relations have reached a state of disrepair which makes a thorough overhaul essential. The difference is that the two academics believe that the unions can reform themselves. Unfortunately the unions are stalemated: lacking the imagination, or the courage, or the organisation, or even the control, to do the job themselves. Put bluntly, they are too weak.

Nor is there any evidence to suggest that management will be able to provoke or persuade the unions to reform. This book deliberately concentrates on trade unions, which could be taken to imply that they are in greater need of reform than management itself. Nothing could be further from the truth. Industrial relations is about the relationship between management and the workers they employ, and if the system has broken down, management must bear just as much responsibility as the unions. Indeed, since many managers are fond of talking about management's right to manage, this suggests that the major responsibility lies with them. But when employers start talking about 'management prerogatives', they are using the rhetoric of industrial relations. As Mr Flanders and Mr Fox rightly point out, 'Most British employers have relied far too long and far too much on union leaders to solve their problems for them.' Most union leaders today are, of course, incapable of doing so.

The case for reform is irresistible, and if neither the unions nor management can undertake it, then the Government must. Clearly the time has come for a Government to reassert its Parliamentary authority over one of the greatest constituent parts of the community it represents and governs. As we have seen, the House of Commons abdicated its responsibility in 1906, and again in 1969. But because it has done so twice, it need not do so a third time.

Reform would certainly involve legislation of a kind which no British parliament has passed, yet is there any reason why it should not be considered? Trade union legislation is not beyond the constitutional power of Parliament, and the system forces a Government which introduces successful legislation to present itself to the electors within five years of doing so. If the electors do not like it, they can throw the Government out. But the passage of such legislation would be based on the conviction that the unions have become a disorderly element in the community, and Parliament would be helping the community by intervening to make collective bargaining rather less disorderly.

The unions are only one of the significant pressure groups in a plural, and democratic, society, and their individual members must abide by the laws Parliament passes. In 1906 Parliament concluded that the collective bargaining process should stand outside the law. If, during the 1970s, Parliament were to change its mind and conclude that the framework of labour law should be imposed on the unions, and if the unions continued to behave as if they were still immune from the law, then the situation would have changed absolutely. By mounting the considerable resources of a vast pressure group with the object of by-passing Parliament, they would have created a semi-revolutionary situation. That would be uncharacteristic of the unions, and is unlikely to happen.

But once a Government acts courageously and begins the business of reform, it is faced with a basic dilemma: should its reforms be designed to make the unions stronger or weaker? The Labour Party concluded in 1969 that the unions were too weak and should be strengthened; the Conservatives, in their policy statements, imply that the unions are too strong and must be weakened. The Labour view is right. There are innumerable arguments for a strong trade union movement, but in a plural society the strongest is that to allow such a vital pressure group to atrophy is dangerous to the physique, and eventually the constitution, of the society. But there are more prosaic arguments in favour of strong trade unions too, best stated as long ago as 1903 by Professor W. J. Ashley, whose description of the dilemma this involves is quoted by Messrs Flanders and Fox.

'The only practical alternative to strikes–peaceful collective bargaining–depends for its efficiency on strongly organised unions,' said Professor Ashley. 'But strongly organised unions, though they are indispensable instruments for enforcing treaties, are powerful weapons of attack.... This puts the employer in an awkward moral situation: it is almost more than can be asked of average human nature to demand that he shall rejoice at the growing power of a union; and yet unless it is strong, it cannot effectively maintain the peace.' This is undeniably true, and time has added a rider to the argument. If the employers have relied on unions to solve their problems for them, they can hardly complain now if the Government decides to undertake a policy which will strengthen the unions.

No Government can begin the process of change, however, without first deciding what it believes the purpose of trade unions to be. Difficult as a redefinition of the unions' role is, it is an essential preliminary to reform.

To start at the beginning: trade unions are representative institutions. The members choose to join a union and they elect the men who lead them; they can leave the union if it does not suit them, and throw out their elected officials. To cast back to the simple definition offered by the Solicitor-General in 1906, 'A trade union is more like a public meeting than a railway company.'

Admittedly, a majority of Britain's trade unions are not strongly representative. Their branch meetings are ill-attended, and will remain so until the meetings are held on the factory floor. But there is no reason why ill-attendance should always be the case. Worker participation in trade unionism is not just 'a good thing', it is essential if the unions are to overcome their weakness. As representative institutions, their membership is their strength, and if the membership is bored or alienated, the union will be weak. The fact is that many unions have become like very poorly-attended public meetings, which suggests that the elected leadership is no longer responsive to the needs of its members, and that the members are too apathetic to throw them out.

Because of this, the unions need prodding from outside to encourage change. A by-product of their weakness is that many unions are run by small cabals, some militant in theory, but all conservative by nature. Being securely established, they naturally resist proposals which could unseat them – another powerful argument for Government intervention.

The process of definition is made easier by establishing what the unions should *not* be trying to do. Clearly the first role to go is that of the union as benefit society. In the past 25 years a whole battery of social service payments have overtaken the minimal benefits which diminutive union dues make possible: today there are wage-related unemployment and sickness benefits, improved pensions, compulsory redundancy payments, and retraining grants, so that the State supports a union member and his family far more effectively than the union can. Sometimes State payments are still not high enough: minimum statutory redundancy payments, in particular, are often a poor reward for years of service. But the way to overcome this problem is not by internally financed funds. It is for the unions to use their bargaining power to persuade the employer to subsidise social services–in the same way that America's United Auto Workers contrives to negotiate remarkably high lay-off pay for its members.

There still remains a fundamental confusion among union leaders over their own role. The leaders of many unions–including the two largest in the country–believe that their job is not just to negotiate for their members, but to change society. This is unreal. It is the job of Governments to change society. Nevertheless, leaders at all levels of the movement persuade themselves that the unions can transform British politics, and they concentrate their energies on verbal critiques of the miserable position of the working man in a mixed economy. In a curious way, this sometimes reduces the capacity for radical thought about the conditions in the world in which the members live–and the members are, after all, primarily interested in just that. Political activity can, and does, reduce the leaders' effectiveness as collective bargainers. It always seemed significant that the Communist leadership of the ETU was never very effective at its task of negotiating good wages for its members. The leaders obviously had other problems to detain them.

The unions always have been, and will remain, social institutions, deeply concerned with Government policy, especially economic policy. But something is missing at the moment. To adapt Dean Acheson, they have lost a mission and have not found a role. Most of their social demands have been met by successive Governments, but no new set of priorities has replaced the old. The old wariness is so deeply entrenched that the unions find it difficult to believe that the old social priorities are redundant; and they have become obsessed with the fear that full employment might suddenly cease to be a reality.

It is of course possible that the commonly accepted assumption that full employment (on the Beveridge scale, which is defined as being less than three per cent of the labour force unemployed) is now an absolute condition of economic policy, will one day come under attack. As social security improved, the Labour Government's determination to keep employment full did waver slightly. Mr Enoch Powell and his rump of Tory supporters would put it seriously at risk if they were able to persuade the majority of the party to accept their belief in the free operation of the laws of supply and demand. But it is wasteful for the unions to gird their loins now for a battle which may never be fought. At present they are simply tilting at windmills.

Consideration of the roles the unions need to play leaves, by process of elimination, a broad definition of their most fruitful task. This is collective bargaining in the economic system as it is, for their members are primarily interested in higher wages and better conditions. Nor is this surprising. Throughout broad areas of British industry wages are low and conditions poor. In fact, one of the reasons why groups of local bargainers have established so much power is that few unions have been able to negotiate pay and conditions at national level which bear any relation either to work done or the financial needs of the family. Only locally have the unions been strong. And, paradoxically, the weakness of the national unions means that to give the appearance of strength they have to lend their name and reputation to the actions of locally-based power groups within the union–a tactic at which both the TGWU and the AEF are becoming increasingly adept.

The inequalities of local bargaining power mean that the weak get weaker and relatively poorer, while the strong get stronger and relatively richer; and the Labour Government's bumbling attempts at an incomes policy have only contributed to this trend. As differentials between groups of workers increased–and they have increased within single plants as well as between different industries–so has tension within the system of industrial relations. Indeed, Mr Flanders and Mr Fox believe that these growing differentials among working men and women are a major factor inducing breakdown in the system as a whole. 'The advantage gained by a strong group', they write, 'may be at the absolute or relative expense of weak groups, who are more likely to be wage-earners than employers, managers or shareholders.'

If the unions are to become stronger, by achieving an admirable balance between local bargaining power and central responsibility, they must deliver the goods more effectively to members at all wage levels, from lowest to highest.

Indeed, if the Government is going to intervene in collective bargaining, it could well start at the lowest wage levels by legislating for the introduction of equal pay for women, which would be a frontal attack on the problem of low pay. And despite the bland dismissals which the subject receives among Government officials, it is worth thinking seriously about a national minimum wage. The introduction of legislation raising the lowest levels of pay need not detract from the unions' role as negotiator. On the contrary, it would give the unions a definite level at which to start negotiations for those who remain outside the unions, and are often very poorly paid. If equal pay and a minimum wage were to act as an impetus to greater organisation, they would attack one of the sources of union weakness–a patchy membership.

The problem of very low pay is, however, not the major one. The greatest single problem confronting the British industrial relations system is the absence of a general method of getting higher pay, equitably distributed, justified by higher productivity, and with some kind of peace obligation on the unions which would not interfere with their basic right to strike. The British strike problem is one in which small groups abuse their power, and the object in solving it is to return the strike to its proper place in the armoury of industrial relations; for use as a final sanction when all else has failed.

I believe that the best, possibly the only, way of achieving all this is by American-style contracts, which bind employer and union to a joint local agreement for a fixed term of between one and three years. This in itself demands an initiative from the government, for the binding agreement is illegal in Britain. Section 4 of the Trade Union Act, 1871, states quite explicitly that: 'Nothing in this Act shall enable any court to entertain any legal proceeding instituted with the object of directly enforcing or recovering damages for the breach of any of the following agreements', and it then goes on to detail virtually every kind of agreement that a union could make, including an agreement between one trade union and another. By definition an employers' association is a trade union and so an agreement between a trade union and an employers' association cannot be enforced. This provision of the 1871 Act would have to be repealed or amended.

But the existing state of hostile intransigence among the unions suggests that this simple Act would not be enough. Although some trade union leaders recognise the value of an all-embracing contract which contains annual increases in wages and improvement in conditions, as well as procedures which restrain, the current trend makes the inclusion of any curbs on the right to strike more, rather than less, difficult. The most senior Transport and General Workers Union officials, when they met their counterparts from the UAW late in July 1969, were enamoured of the theory of the American-style contract, yet only two weeks earlier Jack Jones had ordered all his officials to renegotiate any agreement with the suspicion of a 'penalty clause' in it. The Government, therefore, will have to push the unions in the right direction, for they do not always know what is best for them, and must sometimes be told. It smells of paternalism, but it is unavoidable if the Government is to help them to be strong.

So I would propose the establishment of a Board or Commission, based on the Commission on Industrial Relations (CIR), but with the powers and responsibilities of the American National Labour Relations Board, to overcome the problem created by the unimaginative immobility of vast sections of the trade union movement. The new body could retain the title of the CIR, for its first task would have a distant relationship to one of the jobs now being performed by the hollower CIR established by Mrs Barbara Castle early in 1969. The Government was then empowered to request that all large companies register their collective agreements with the Department of Employment and Productivity; the Government could then refer the worst of them to the CIR for investigation. But the remodelled CIR ought to be a much more ambitious operation: it should be empowered to demand that all companies now registering agreements with the DEP make a contract with the unions they recognise. Next the CIR should state that the compulsory contract would, after a fixed period of time, become legally binding on both sides.

It is no use, as the Conservatives suggest, making all agreements legally binding at one fell swoop, since most of the agreements in British industry are not worthy of the name. They are either contained in volumes of minutes of a works committee, like the agreements at the GEC-English Electric Trafford Park factories in Manchester, or they are written on three of four ill-considered sheets of foolscap paper. Codification in a contract would necessarily lead to renegotiation, and substantial changes in the practice of industrial relations could be made during that period of renegotiation.

There is one additional point here, however. The Tory proposal that unions should be allowed to negotiate themselves out of a binding contract would have to be resisted. The strongest local groups, who sometimes abuse their power and remove themselves from the mainstream of union activity, are among those the contract is intended to control: they are the people who will have the bargaining power to reject the binding element in any contract they would negotiate. And the major purpose of the contract is to impose a greater degree of control in return for higher wages and better working conditions.

If the contract were to become the new basis of industrial relations in Britain, what would be its advantages, and how would it work? Curiously, that apotheosis of the voluntary system, the Donovan Commission report, gave one of the best reasons in favour of the contract when it explained that the British system of negotiation provides no way of linking levels of pay to the efficiency of companies. 'Thus change becomes the subject of dispute and controversy, and is too often as a result delayed, or not even attempted,' the report stated. Clearly the only sound method of paying higher wages is higher production, and the contract undeniably aids the introduction of technological innovations and investment programmes which make this possible.

It has other advantages too. By negotiating a factory-wide, or company-embracing contract, the likelihood of less powerful groups or workers being discriminated against is reduced. The existence of an agreed, written contract is also an incentive to management to let the unions help enforce it with a system of full-time, shop stewards. The contract will also inevitably contain procedures forbidding lightning unofficial strikes, but the contract should also make them unnecessary.

If this sounds rather bald, there are more subtle advantages to the contract too. These are best illustrated by the fact that the American GEC company avoids signing contracts with unions whenever it can: its management have concluded that the contract makes the union too strong and too intrusive. Nor is it difficult to see why, for it obviously curbs 'management prerogatives' just as it curbs the unlimited right to strike. Disciplinary action cannot be taken unilaterally, nor can significant decisions about investment programmes which will change work patterns within the factory; nor can overtime working begin without consultation. Indeed, a complex pattern of consultation procedures, demanding both professionalism and commitment from union officials, is one of the attractions of the contract.

In itself, consultation strengthens the union, and, in turn, it should increase the interest of rank and file members on the shop floor. When their working lives are directly affected by union negotiation, and branch meetings are held in the factory (as they must be), the likelihood of their participating directly in the affairs of the union is much greater. And, if that is the case, they are less likely to complain at another common clause in the contract: that union dues are deducted by the employer at source. Check-off, as this is called, boosts union funds by making it impossible for members to wriggle out of paying dues.

Such a major alteration to the traditional way of doing things would be as great a test of management as of the unions. Indeed, since management would have to initiate many of the changes, and calculate how they might be paid for, their challenge would be even greater. At the moment few organisations on either side of industry would be capable of implementing the changes demanded by the contract, which is one good reason for a time-lag before it becomes legally binding.

The functions of the new CIR would not stop at the order to make binding contracts. Its staff would have to see that all contracts met an agreed standard (to prevent two unenthusiastic parties making a contract saying that, in effect, there would be no contract). Arguments will inevitably follow about the interpretation of even the best-drafted contracts: disputes will arise about the actual working of consultation procedures, for a contract cannot cover every eventuality. The CIR must be well enough staffed, with enough local offices, to provide rapid arbitration. It could incorporate some classic features of the Swedish system, in which arbitration is a deliberately speedy process–for delay and its frustrations are one of the most convincing explanations for the rash of unofficial strikes in Britain.

Alternatively, the contract itself could contain clauses proposing binding independent arbitration, especially over issues like discipline, where employer and union do not agree. An independent arbiter could also perform the role I have delegated to the CIR–settling interpretation disputes. Independent arbitration has never been common in Britain, but in a society which accepts quasi-judicial processes with such equanimity, there is no reason why not.

Nor is there any really sound reason why substantive agreements about wages and conditions should not be allied to procedural agreements. The Conservative Party believes the two should be independent of each other; but why should negotiated annual wage increases and fringe benefits in a contract not persuade men who benefit by them to adhere to the procedural sections in the same contract?

The notion of men failing to keep to procedures leads inexorably on to the most troublesome question of all: what is to be done about the small groups of men who stubbornly ignore the terms of the contract forbidding unofficial strikes, and down tools without warning, bringing production to a halt, disrupting production schedules and putting their colleagues out of work?

The single objection which emerged most clearly from the great dispute over the Industrial Relations Bill in 1969 was that the unions will never willingly accept a framework of law which ends with individual strikers being taken to court and fined. And it is, I believe, useless to construct a system which contains provisions of this kind. An alternative is not easy to come by, yet some kind of deterrent to flagrant breaches of a contract is unavoidable.

As the new legal framework will include statutory protection for working men and women against summary dismissal (with a quasi-judicial system operated by the CIR to hear appeals from those who believe they have been unfairly dismissed, when the contract itself does not cover the case), I suggest that any workers who break the contract by striking unofficially, immediately lose their protection against summary dismissal. An employer would have the secure knowledge that he could dismiss identifiable trouble-makers and reduce tension with his own industrial relations system. It would effectively deter many would-be renegades, for few men willingly surrender their job, even when employment is relatively easy to find–for one thing, social security is less easily come by for a man who has lost his job for disciplinary reasons.

But the framework must also contain some protection for an employer who sacks the leaders of an unofficial strike, for the deterrent would be a poor thing if a union could then simply call out all its members in that factory. It would be necessary to remove the union's protection from immunity granted under the 1906 Act, in the case of a union which deliberately ignored the contract and used its authority to call a lengthy strike on behalf of men who had been justifiably dismissed. Once the unions' immunity was gone, the employer could then sue for damages, and the damages should bear some relation to the financial losses suffered by the company during the illegal strike.

It could lead to a situation described by John L. Lewis, the American Mineworkers' leader, who was once asked how he valued his chances after a judge's summing-up in a case in which the union had broken a contract. 'He's in his room', said John L., 'writing his judgement on an adding machine.' The Mineworkers had to pay a fine of more than a million dollars; and fines on much the same scale would have to be levied here, in the extreme circumstances I have described, if the law were to deter unions from irresponsibly helping men who had themselves behaved irresponsibly.

This proposal is fraught with pitfalls. To begin with, it would alter quite fundamentally the relationship between the unions and the Courts, but it would do so only in extremes cases. The object of the contract is to prevent occurrences of this kind, and, like most deterrents, this one is placed in the framework in the hope that there will be no need to use it. The deterrent would, of course, apply to an employer too, and the law should contain punitive damages for a man who has been unfairly sacked, under the guise of legal summary dismissal.

For the rest, unconstitutional action officially undertaken by a union in defiance of the contract, could be taken by an employer to the courts as a simple breach of contract case: and the reverse is equally true. But since the contract would contain, as American contracts do, conditions under which a strike is legal and methods by which it can justifiably be undertaken, there should be no reason why either party to the agreement should need to act unconstitutionally.

One problem remains: what is to be done about economically damaging strikes which occur quite legally when negotiations to renew the contract break down? These are the strikes which, in the United States, the Taft–Hartley 90-day cooling off period is specifically designed to prevent. The temptation is to do the same in Britain, but this, I think, would be a mistake. If there are damaging official strikes at the end of a contract, that will be one of the drawbacks of an improved, but still imperfect, system. Peace-making in these disputes would be of the traditional variety, with the DEP conciliation machine moving in to try to solve them.

There would, however, be a case for using a cooling-off period in those areas of British industry which were not immediately covered by a contract. Since the CIR will have to confine its attention to larger companies for a few years at least, there will be many small, but nevertheless economically significant, companies where a stoppage could have unfortunate multiplying effects. It is possible that the existence of reserve cooling off powers in these areas (to be applied by the CIR rather than the DEP), would act as an incentive to both management and labour in small companies, to start contract-making.

One of the reasons why the appeal of cooling-off powers itself cooled during 1969, was that the civil servants who would have had to use them turned cold at the thought of imposing them in the docks. American experience shows that Taft–Hartley simply does not work on the waterfront; the dockers just strike 90 days later than they intended. The docks in America, as in Britain, are a unique problem, and their industrial relations are significantly worse than in other industries. So there is a natural tendency to conclude that special measures, including compulsory arbitration, should be imposed on dockland. This would, I believe, be a mistake possibly a disastrous one. The contract is flexible enough to apply in the docks too, and the new scheme would contain a deterrent (summary dismissal), which does not exist now.

Clearly, to allow management and labour on the docks to make binding contracts, the National Dock Labour Scheme would have to be amended to give the Dock Labour Boards disciplinary functions which embrace the right to summary dismissal when necessary. While the amendment is going through, it might be an opportune moment to introduce independent arbitration to the docks, to replace the internal compulsory arbitration system in which each side is equally represented. This would, at least, end the stalemate which stultifies any attempt to change patterns of behaviour among the most anxious, insecure and difficult section of the country's labour force.

But could the unions, never mind management, make the contract system work? The answer at this moment is clear from the preceding chapters: they could not. The object of the scheme, however, is not simply to restore order and strengthen the unions. It assumes that the unions cannot become stronger until they have re-organised, and a further object of the contract system is to persuade them to do just this.

The greatest initial problem is that British management, unlike their American counterparts, would have to negotiate contracts with more than one union. In America the concept of the single bargaining agent, in which only one union is granted the right to negotiate with each employer on behalf of all the employees, was introduced 35 years ago when the unions were just beginning to take a grip on the economy. In Britain the principle would come too late to have the same impact as it did in America, but this does not mean it could not be introduced here, however gradually. The powers of the CIR would include the right to hear appeals from unions which have been refused recognition, and it would be allowed, as Mrs Castle's White Paper proposed, to make an order demanding that an employer recognise a union which could prove it had substantial membership. There is no good reason why they should not, in these cases, apply the principle of the single bargaining agent, and grant recognition to only one union, to bargain for all, where more than one union is competing for recognition.

This would be a start, but even more drastic internal union reorganisation would be necessary if the unions were to become as strong as the proposed contract system would allow them to. It is, however, too late to expect the longed-for German and Swedish industrial unions to emerge suddenly, and contrary to all trends. The clumsy, haphazard structure of the British trade union movement is a permanent characteristic, something to be made the best of, even if it is not always easy to find a way.

The General and Municipal Workers' Union does offer a theoretical solution; its concentration on the idea of strong trade groups in a general union with a powerful and able administration, is the most attractive blueprint for the future. If this were to become common, there could be a membership explosion, largely through amalgamations, in the Transport and General Workers Union, and the GMWU; and the AEF could swallow its pride and become a more general craftsmen's union.

The white-collar workers are a rather different case (and they will become increasingly important as recognition becomes easier for unions to achieve). All the largest unions woke up to the membership potential among white-collar workers too late, and by the time they had seen the light, the Association of Scientific, Technical and Managerial Staffs had already begun to benefit from the steady membership growth which had been available to any union showing interest. Their vision ought to be rewarded, and the ASTMS should become the general white-collar workers' union.

If the big unions do develop a voracious appetite for small unions, and can overcome the pride of the leaders and members of these smaller unions by offering such improved services that the results show in higher wages, their very size will begin to solve some of the problems of multi-unionism in Britain's factories. Once they are big enough, and secure enough, to stop looking over their shoulders at the union next door, they might initiate their own rationalisation process. In plants in which one union's membership was in a minority, it might become willing to swap those members, and take over others belonging to a rival union in another factory. Membership swapping is almost as effective a way of reducing multi-unionism as amalgamation. The trouble is that no union yet feels strong enough to indulge in it.

But greater strength cannot be based only on a larger membership; there must be higher dues to get enough men, and higher salaries to get the right men. Higher dues are, if nothing else, a symbol of the members' right to high-quality services from a well-trained, well paid research staff and an efficient business organisation. To beat the big corporations, a union must model some of its activities on the corporation–an idea which has so far been anathema to the British movement.

As for the working officials, higher salaries might well improve their quality too, for the wages paid by many unions stretch the loyalty of men who might want to work for the unions rather too far. And a radical improvement in the quality of officials is clearly a necessary preliminary to the members respecting the union.

If this scheme were to be implemented, and the unions were to become stronger, however, there would be an even better case than there is now for safeguarding the rights of individual members. The unions themselves should, of course, be sufficiently confident to establish individual arbitration machinery for individual complaints against the union. But even if they were to do this, it would not be enough, for many complaints against unions come from men who are debarred from joining, and who, when they wish to work in a closed shop, find this reduces their chances of employment.

The Donovan Report proposed that an independent review body be attached to the office of the Registrar of Trade Unions, with the right to hear cases from working men who believed they had been unfairly discriminated against by unions. This is an admirable idea, except that I would attach the review body to the CIR, with the same emphasis here on speed as in its other spheres of activity.

This, then, is my list of proposals. They cannot be complete, but their purpose is to indicate a change in the direction of industrial relations rather than to provide a detailed blueprint. Nevertheless, the plan outlines a series of far reaching reforms, in which the Government, through Parliament, would reassert its authority over the process of collective bargaining after more than half a century of neglect. The Government has already intervened in other fields, and many of its moves have palpably assisted the trade union movement and its members–in employment policy, in subsidies to declining industries and to companies locating in areas of high unemployment, and in financing better social services through higher taxation. There is no reason why the unions themselves should remain immune any longer.

To sum up, the scheme embraces the creation of a powerful new state institution built upon the CIR to help weak unions become stronger and more responsive to their members' wishes, and to check the power of the strongest groups of trade unionists. Even so, the employers would still be the major countervailing power. The system would acknowledge the spread of local bargaining, and both control and institutionalise it by means of the binding contract; it would also include a deterrent to prevent abuse of the collective bargaining machinery by irresponsible groups of trade unionists.

It would, of course, be costly: there is no denying that one of the major attractions of the contract for the unions is that it can be used to push wages levels steadily upwards. The price of an end to disorder would be high–incalculably high, because it is impossible to estimate the extent to which management could absorb the wages-cost in the increased productivity which the contract ought to make possible.

But this should not act as a brake on the programme. Britain will be burdened by debt for some years to come, and the nation's overseas creditors should be persuaded that both the cost and the short-term industrial problems which would inevitably follow should be seen as part of a longer-term programme to stabilise the whole British economy, not just the trade union movement. It would not please the speculators, and Britain's balance of payments might relapse briefly: but if the international creditors are genuinely interested in the restoration of economic order, they should be sympathetic towards the objectives of these proposals.

To conclude, my scheme is liberal reformist in intent, even though it might not appear so at first glance to many who call themselves by that name. The object of the scheme is in the best liberal tradition: it is designed to prevent chaos. And if Mr Flanders and Mr Fox are right–as I believe they are–the system of industrial relations is in grave danger of collapsing into disorder.

There is something even more fundamental than this. The fact that the liberal tradition is under attack lends an urgency to the need for radically new proposals to reform industrial relations. Liberalism, like any other political creed, demands constant redefinition if it is to keep pace with shifting circumstances. There was a time when the liberal attitude towards trade unionism left the unions to their own devices. But the changes undergone by the unions during the past generation have brought about a prospect of chaos: and when that threatens, it is time to redefine the liberal attitude.

But let there be no illusions about the scheme I propose. It would be strenuously resisted by powerful unions (though less grimly than might at first seem likely), and I would not envy the proposer of these reforms who had to stare into the whites of Hugh Scanlon's, Jack Jones's and Victor Feather's eyes. The imposition of the system could lead to traumatic short-term economic problems before the adjustments were made, and the number of strikes might well temporarily increase before it began to ebb. It would not solve the present problems of British industrial relations before a decade was out; indeed, it could be a generation before the new system finally settled down. But it shows me a light at the end of the tunnel, and I cannot see one now.

A Note on Sources

The basic source for this book is my week-to-week contact with trade unionists. The material is a product of a thousand conversations, interviews, and arguments with men who earn their living doing the job I write about. It would be impossible to credit them all; not just because of number of people involved, but because many trade unionists speak freely only when they are sure they will not be quoted. It seems that some of them are unfortunately never credited with their own bright ideas.

But it would be quite wrong not to credit authors of published work on which I have drawn, and I do so here, chapter-by-chapter. The works referred to have often been used in more than one chapter. I have mentioned them in the chapter in which they are most often used.

CHAPTER 1: The historical description of the Trades Disputes Bill is from volumes of Hansard from April to December 1906, containing the protracted debates, and from files of *The Times* for 1906. I also drew on the monumental *History of Trade Unionism* by Sidney and Beatrice Webb (Longmans, Green, 1920), and sought legal guidance from the standard work, *Citrine's Trade Union Law*, 3rd Edition, by M. A. Hickling (Stevens, 1957).

CHAPTER 2: The narrative describing the relationship between trade unions and the Government was helped by *A Short History of the TUC*, by John Lovell and B. C. Roberts (Macmillan, 1968), and the facts came from Government publications, especially the *Employment and Productivity Gazette*, an invaluable publication issued monthly by the Department of Employment and Productivity, and the Trade and Navigation Accounts.

CHAPTER 3: The opening argument is stimulated by Professor H. A. Turner's pamphlet, *Is Britain Really Strike Prone?*, an occasional paper from the University of Cambridge Department of Applied Economics (Cambridge University Press, 1969); it is again helped by statistics from the *Employment and Productivity Gazette*, and by the Report of the Court of Inquiry into a Dispute between Girling Limited, Bromborough, and members of the AEF or the ASTMS, published in December 1968. I was also greatly helped by loans of the complete, unpublished transcript of the Court's proceedings by the DEP and the ASTMS. George Woodcock's radio broadcast was published in *The Listener* in December 1959.

CHAPTER 4: The annual Congress Reports of the Trades Union Congress, published each year by the TUC are an invaluable refresher for old, and sometimes inaccurate memories. Mr Woodcock's quoted remarks are from the same broadcast mentioned above.

CHAPTER 5: The AEF Rule Book is published by the AEF, Peckham Road, London, and I have used the latest issue revised after the Rules Revision Meeting in 1965. An article in *Management Today*, May 1969, called 'Impasse Among the Engineers', by Jim Daly, was another useful source for this chapter. The Rules of the General and Municipal Workers Union are published by the GMWU, Ruxley Towers, Esher, Surrey. Material for the section on shop stewards was drawn mainly from two research papers written for the Royal Commission on Trade Unions and Employers' Associations–Research Paper 1, 'The role of Shop Stewards in British Industrial Relations', by W. E. J. McCarthy, and Research Paper 10, 'Shop Stewards and Workshop Relations', by W. E. J. McCarthy and S. R. Parker, both published by the Stationery Office. *Shop Stewards in British Industry*, by J. F. B. Goodman and T. G. Whittingham (McGraw Hill, 1969) was also useful.

CHAPTER 6: The basic sources for this chapter are the published proposals for reform by each of the protagonists in the argument: *The Royal Commission on Trade Unions and Employers' Associations, 1965–68, Report* (Command 3623); the Government White Paper, *In Place of Strife*, published in January 1969; the Conservative policy document, *Fair Deal at Work*, published by Conservative Central Office in 1968; and *Programme for Action*, published by the TUC in June 1969. I also used Clive Jenkins's and J. E. Mortimer's book, *The Kind of Laws the Unions Ought to Want* (Pergamon, 1968).

CHAPTER 7: The major published source for this chapter is articles in a volume in the Penguin Modern Management Series called *Collective Bargaining*, edited by Allan Flanders. I made particular use of three of its chapters: J. E. Isaac on 'Compulsory Arbitration in Australia'; T. L. Johnston on 'The Bargaining Process in Sweden'; and the introductory essay by Mr Flanders himself, 'The Nature of Collective Bargaining'. A publication of the National Labour Relations Board in Washington called *A Layman's Guide to Basic Law under the National Labour Relations Act* was also valuable.

CHAPTER 8: The essay by Allan Flanders and Alan Fox, called 'The Reform of Collective Bargaining: from Donovan to Durkheim', was published in the *British Journal of Industrial Relations*, Vol. VII, No. 2, July 1969.

Index

INDEX